CALLED
Together

DOROTHY LANGSTAFF

WITH ALAN LANGSTAFF

DEDICATION

This book is dedicated to my beloved husband, Alan, my wonderful life partner in marriage and ministry, and to our children and grandchildren. God's Word says,

"Tell your children about it,
Let your children tell their children,
And their children another generation."
Joel 1:3

We leave this testimony as a legacy to our daughters, Beth and Joy, who are gifts from God; to our precious grandchildren, Mitchel, Jessica, Timothy, Jonathan, Hayley, and Benjamin; and to all our spiritual sons and daughters.

IMPOSSIBLE. DIFFICULT. DONE!

It was in 1975, when a visiting speaker called me forward and asked, "Has God been talking to you about writing a book?" He went on to say, "Begin to write immediately. It is needed yesterday!"

It wasn't until 1980 that God confirmed this word to my heart and I began to write this book.

This assignment from God has been like running a long marathon with many obstacles to overcome along the way. Due to many physical challenges, including a sprained right arm and damaged vision, the task seemed almost impossible. I was encouraged to persevere when I read Bob Gass' words, "The battle is always over your future. Satan's strategy is to destroy the author and the book will never be born."

I gained courage from the writings of a great man of God, Hudson Taylor, who had three words to describe a challenging assignment:

"Impossible. Difficult. Done!"

By the grace of God and the help of my husband Alan and other wonderful people, I have been able to persevere through the impossible and the difficult, until finally I can say, "The book is done!"

ACKNOWLEDGEMENTS

Many people have encouraged me along the way. My deepest appreciation goes to . . .

My husband, Alan, without whom this book would not have been possible. He believed in me, supported me, and prayed for me, and made an essential contribution to the writing of our story. For tireless hours patiently read the manuscript to me, correcting, and rewriting. It has been such a blessing to relive our experiences together, sometimes in laughter and tears. We realized once more how great and faithful is our God and what a wonderful life He has given us together.

Our daughter, Beth, who right back at the beginning, painstakingly and patiently coached me. Refusing to write it for me, she would say, "You have to do it in your own words." She has spent countless hours reading the manuscript, editing and correcting. It's true to say the book would not have been written without her help and encouragement.

Our daughter, Joy, who was the God-given answer to our prayer, being the first one to put the initial manuscript on computer. She had difficulty concentrating as she became so engrossed in what she was reading and remarked, "This is great. When are you going to finish it so I can read the rest of the story?" She was a constant source of support along the way.

Elizabeth Wright who, in November 2007, when she knew I was writing a book, challenged me saying, "When are you going to finish it? You need to set a goal. How about six months for the first draft and 12 months to finish it? You can do it!" This was confirmed immediately by Alan when he told me we had to finish it by November 2008 in time to celebrate my 70th birthday and our 50th wedding anniversary.

Ron Olson, who worked so hard putting the final manuscript on the computer as I finished each chapter, using his skills to correct and adjust it. He patiently worked with me, putting the book together and helping me to make countless decisions before finally sending it to the publisher. His help and advice were invaluable.

Suzann Beck, with her wonderful gifts and talents, who designed the book cover. She also gave me valuable counsel and insight, and spent hours and hours reading the manuscript, editing and correcting.

Beth Bentley, who took time to read the manuscript and made this comment, "I love the book. I felt that as I read it, you opened up your life and invited me in to sit and hear about the wonderful things that the Lord has done for you. I was encouraged and challenged."

June Coxhead, who wrote the first story of The Temple Trust for *Vision Magazine.*

Nancy Shea, who was the very first one to type the manuscript in its early stages.

Jim Spillman, who first brought the word of the Lord that I was to write a book. He planted the seed.

Michael Harper and *Dick Mills,* who confirmed that word and encouraged me to write our story from my perspective.

Myles Munroe, who urged me to write when I heard him say, "Don't die with a book in you."

Finally, to those who prayed for me during this long process, and those who God used to encourage and affirm me when I felt inadequate for the task, I am very grateful.

TABLE OF CONTENTS

THE VISION UNFOLDS

THE MINISTRY GROWS

A NEW DAY

INTRODUCTION

Dorothy and I had the privilege of living through the days of the Charismatic Renewal, the greatest move of God in the twentieth century. It was what I call "a decade of destiny." It is hard for people living more than a generation later to realize how significant that time was. My longtime friend and Pentecostal leader, David Cartledge, once told me that in 1969 the Pentecostal Church in Australia was as "as dead as a doornail." With few exceptions, most Pentecostal and Evangelical churches were not large or growing significantly. All that changed in the 1970s as a new foundation was laid for what is happening now. We often forget how far the church has come.

We had the God-given opportunity thrust upon us to lead The Temple Trust during that decade. From small beginnings it grew to become the major renewal ministry in Australia, and went on to touch the nation for God. It brought together people of all different denominations and streams in a remarkable expression of cooperation and unity, culminating in the Jesus '79 Conference—the largest Charismatic gathering in Australia up until that time. The evening meetings were held at the Randwick Racecourse because there was no building in Sydney large enough to hold the crowds of fifteen to twenty thousand people. After that event I said, "The day will come when there will be a church in Australia with more people in it than there is at this Conference." That has since come to pass with Hillsong Church in Sydney.

Many people do not realize that, although I was the leader of The Temple Trust, Dorothy and I founded it together. We have been a team all through the years. We were "called together." Dorothy was an integral and essential part of all that happened. She was not only a partner in marriage and ministry, she was co-founder of The Temple Trust and a member of the Board of Directors. More than that, she was the one who interceded and prayed, the one who had a heart for unity in the Body of Christ, the one who believed in me before I believed in myself. Without her I could not have accomplished what I did during those days.

It is only fitting that Dorothy, who was right at the heart of all that was happening, should write this story from her perspective. Consequently, it needs to be stated that this is neither a history of the Charismatic Renewal in Australia, nor the complete story of The Temple Trust. Because of the personal nature of this story, many friends, ministers, co-workers, and people that labored with us during those years from so many different churches and ministries, are not mentioned by name. We do, however, thank God for each and every one of them, and remember with gratitude all that we shared together in those years.

This story is a personal testimony of our adventures in life and ministry as we sought to follow in faith and obedience the voice of the Lord. The story is woven around the events of that "decade of destiny," and is a testimony to an awesome and faithful God who called us together to serve Him.

I am so grateful to God that Dorothy has poured herself into writing this book. It has been a monumental task, made even more strenuous by the physical limitations she has had to overcome. Dorothy has been my wonderful partner in marriage and ministry and still is to this day. Truly we have been "called together."

Alan Langstaff

A PERSONAL WORD FOR YOU.

It is my prayer that you will meet with God in these pages and that you will be stirred to seek Him and give Him the pages of your life on which to write His will and plan.

You were born for a purpose and have a part to play in history. You are living in a strategic time. Look beyond yourself to see what God sees for you, His Church, and the world.

It is my prayer that you will be spoiled for the ordinary and discover a wonderful life of faith and radical obedience. Whether young or old, it's never too late to become what God has called you to be.

"Call to Me, and I will answer you, and show you
great and mighty things, which you do not know."
Jeremiah 33:3

Dorothy Langstaff

I HAVE A DESTINY

I have a destiny I know I shall fulfill,
I have a destiny in that city on a hill.
I have a destiny and it's not an empty wish,
for I know I was born for such a time as this.

Long before the ages You predestined me
to walk in all the works
You have prepared for me.
You'd given me a part to play in history
to help prepare a bride for eternity.

I did not choose You but You have chosen me,
and appointed me for bearing fruit abundantly.
I know You will complete
the work begun in me,
by the power of Your Spirit working mightily.

Words and Music by Mark Altrogge

PROLOGUE

Chapter 1
Arise, Shine. It's A New Day!

CHAPTER 1

Arise, Shine.
It's A New Day!

"Arise, shine; for your light has come!
And the glory of the Lord is risen upon you."
Isaiah 60:1

"Arise, shine; for your light has come! And the glory of the Lord is risen upon you," (Isaiah 60:1).

What an honor it was to stand before that great gathering and read those prophetic words from scripture—words that were so appropriate, so alive, and so full of hope and challenge.

It was the opening service of the Jesus '79 National Charismatic Conference, held on the steps of the Sydney Opera House. At least ten thousand people from all over Australia and beyond were gathered together, giving glory to Jesus on this beautiful Sunday afternoon in January.

Heavy rain had been falling in Sydney and many people had prayed there would be fine weather during the opening service and the conference meetings to follow. God answered the prayers of His people. The day was fine and warm, with a gentle breeze blowing off the Harbour.

What a glorious sight! Many people had colored umbrellas to protect themselves from the sun. The white sails of the Opera House rose majestically behind this great crowd, and the Harbour Bridge, the clear blue sky and the deeper blue of the Harbour formed a dramatic background.

A platform for the speakers, musicians, and special guests had been erected on the lower level facing the Opera House steps. All those seated on it had the thrill of looking at this magnificent sight. Television vans had arrived and news cameramen were busy filming this significant and colorful event. Another film crew was recording scenes for the film "It's a New Day."

The atmosphere was charged with excitement and the anticipation of what God was going to do during this conference. For Alan and me this was the fulfillment of a dream. All the glory of the past Charismatic Renewal and the glory of a new day dawning were culminating in this conference, and a new era was beginning in the times and purposes of God.

The crowd was hushed as Alan gave the keynote address. His prophetic message on the New Day was interrupted by a Russian ship, which heralded its arrival with a loud blast of its horn. It was heard all across the Harbour and seemed to be adding an emphatic "Amen" at just the right moment. The great crowd broke into spontaneous applause and shouts of praise as Alan repeated the phrase, "It's a new day! It's a new day! It's a new day! Hallelujah!"

The moment was not only etched on our memories and viewed with joy from the heavenlies, but a news reporter who sensed the dramatic timing recorded it for the daily paper. The headline read, "RUSSIAN SHIP HERALDS JESUS '79 CONFERENCE."

That afternoon as we looked back on all God had done, and stood on the threshold of the future, we were filled with an awesome sense of destiny. We knew that God had hardly begun to do what He had purposed and planned for this great nation of Australia, part of the lands that explorer de Quiros had boldly proclaimed as the "South Land of the Holy Spirit."

It was the dawning of a new day, not only for Australia, but also for Alan and me, too. God had dramatic changes in store for us. We experienced that deep-down, inexplicable feeling of destiny—the feeling that everything was going according to plan. There was a special part for us to play in history. Even if it was never written in the history books, that part was important to us and to God.

I had sensed the hand of God on my life even as a child. I am sure that it was His perfect plan for me to come to Australia 30 years earlier. I had sailed into the same Sydney Harbour for the first time one misty morning in September 1950.

OUR ROOTS

CHAPTER 2

In The Beginning

"Before I made you in your mother's womb,
I chose you.
Before you were born,
I set you apart for a special work."
Jeremiah 1:5 (NCV)

The sun was warm on my back. The long summer grass waved slightly, stirred by the gentle breeze. I loved being out in the middle of the large field behind our house. The field was the perfect place to play. My brother David and I would make hospitals for wounded butterflies there and run snail races along the wall.

That particular day, I was all by myself. Snuggled down in the grass, I felt as though I was in a secret place where no one could see me. All of a sudden, I became acutely aware of the presence of God. Instantly I felt close and special to Him. I knew He was speaking to me. "I have something very special for you to do when you grow up," He said, although I heard no audible voice. My heart responded without hesitation. "Yes, God!" Even at the age of seven, I knew that my life belonged to Him. I began to understand that there was a call of God on my life. I had been born to fulfill a destiny. I kept that secret all to myself and treasured it in my heart.

I was born in November 1938 in Rhyl, a seaside resort town in North Wales. It was a popular place for city dwellers to escape the hustle and bustle of life in cities like Manchester or Liverpool and, after 1940, the dreaded bombing raids of the Battle of Britain. They could find relief in the fresh sea air, warm sunshine, golden sand and ocean waves. A wide promenade stretched along the beach. Across the road a long row of guesthouses facing the ocean welcomed visitors.

My Scottish parents, Mary and Walter Roan, decided to settle in Rhyl where Dad found work. I was the youngest in a family of four children, the long-awaited daughter after three sons. My parents christened me Dorothy, "gift of God," and received me with joy and thankfulness.

Thinking back, I am very grateful to God for my parents and for all they did for me. Active church members, they introduced me early to the life and fellowship of a small Welsh Congregational church called Tynewydd. A big day in my young life was the first time my brother Alan took me to Sunday School there.

My first years of childhood were lived with the shadow of war over every aspect of life. The focal point of our day was the BBC radio broadcast bringing news of the war. Nobody was allowed to make a single sound during the broadcast. If we did, Dad would reprove us with his familiar "Shhhht!" I could tell it must be something very important. Sometimes I heard the voice of Winston Churchill, Britain's Prime Minister, as he encouraged the British people to be strong and hold fast. His words lifted our spirits and strengthened our faith in eventual victory.

Meanwhile, wartime imposed its patterns on everyday life. Food was scarce and strictly rationed. My brothers and I didn't always appreciate the restrictions. Dad would watch us like a hawk to make sure we spread the butter thinly enough on our bread. Butter wrapping paper and jam jars had to be scraped clean so nothing was wasted. Mum and Dad went without eggs and cheese so that we children would have more at mealtimes. Mum had to save ration coupons to buy something special like jelly or cake for our birthday parties. One afternoon after setting the table, I fancied a "cheese sandwich." I cut two slices of precious cheese and stuck them together with equally precious butter. When my brother John threatened to tell Mum, I was so terrified that I ran upstairs and flushed the cheese down the toilet. I didn't see a banana until I was six, and then my first taste was a disappointment—it had come out of cold storage and was green and firm. I much preferred the bright red juicy apples that I could polish until I could almost see my face in them.

Dad, along with a partner, had his own printing business called The Clywd Press. This meant that we had no shortage of paper, cardboard and note pads. I had a whole drawer in my dressing table filled with a variety of colors and sizes. He sometimes brought work home and I would help him collate or stamp receipts. I particularly loved to help at Christmas time when there were cards to be dusted with silver and gold sparkles. Dad worked long hours. It was a familiar sight to see Mum keeping his dinner hot over a pan of water on the stove.

While younger men were off fighting in the war, older men like Dad served in the Home Guard. He was often on duty at night and on weekends. He would leave the house in his brown uniform with his face and hands smeared with dark brown. One of his jobs was to guard the bombs that had fallen but had not exploded. He would stay until the bomb squad came to render the explosives harmless.

At dusk, Mum would draw the blackout curtains tightly across the windows. Not a chink of light must be visible to the German bombers on their missions of destruction. Many nights they flew directly over Rhyl on their way to Liverpool. We were always relieved to hear the drone of their engines fade away without the ominous whine of falling bombs, and always concerned for those who would be the target of that night's raid.

Not all the enemy bombers made it back to Germany. The planes were shot down and survivors taken prisoner. In our area, they were sent to work on a prison farm on the outskirts of town. Rather awed at first, I got to know one of the "enemy"—a German POW named Herbert. He was granted permission to attend our little church, and he made a rich contribution by playing the organ for our Sunday evening services.

When the nights grew cold, Mum and Dad used to invite him home for a cup of tea. He accepted with pleasure. He clearly enjoyed the warmth of our home and in his broken English he admired my mother's fine china and nice things. I listened intently as he spoke of his family back in Germany and his own disillusionment with war. He didn't want to fight, he said, he simply wanted to live in peace. One Sunday night, he told us that he would not be back again. He was being moved back to Germany. He shook hands with each of us and said, "Bless God You!" The meaning was clear even if the English was muddled. We exchanged several letters with Herbert and sent small packets of things such as sewing needles and cottons that were scarce in post-war Germany. His last letter announced that he was going to South Africa.

War left its mark and its memories. My eldest brother Alan captured many of the memories in watercolors and black ink. Fascinated, I sat and watched him paint for hours, following every brush stroke. I watched so closely that my nose was frequently almost touching the paint. Alan would patiently say, "You have to move back, I can't see what I'm doing."

He was eight years older than I was, and somehow different from my other brothers, John and David. Of course, I had fun playing with them, particularly David, as he was closest to my age. I made a nuisance of myself wanting to play their boy's games. If they condescended to let me join in, I sometimes came off worst. In Cowboys and Indians, they would take me prisoner and tie me up with rope. They hog-tied me so tightly once that they had to fetch Mum, highly displeased, to cut me free with a pair of scissors. Like any brothers with a little sister, they teased me unmercifully. Their favorite nicknames for me were "skeeter bomber," after the aircraft, and "skinny legs."

In spite of the teasing, it was good to have big brothers—especially when some strange boys harassed and bullied me on the way home from school. It was John who came to my rescue and scared them off.

When the other two went off to play cricket and football, leaving me behind, Alan would stay and play with me. In so many ways, he showed me what Jesus was like. In him, I saw the love and the goodness of God.

Early one Wednesday morning, Alan took ill. He woke with pains in his stomach severe enough to summon the doctor immediately.

"It's appendicitis," he said. "His appendix has to come out."

Alan was admitted to the hospital that day. On Thursday morning, he had the operation. Mum visited him soon after. He was still feeling ill, though that was surely natural. A deep depression settled on Mum in spite of all the reassurances that he would be fine.

He would cry out, "The pain is like knives cutting into my stomach."

Later, when the family visited, I sat at the foot of the bed. He pleaded with me, "Please don't bump the bed. It hurts so much."

The sister on duty reassured Mum, "You can go home now. I'll give him an enema, that will fix him."

We all went home, but the worry persisted. Then, at midnight, there was a knocking on our front door. It was a message from the hospital. My parents were to come at once. Dad said he would go. Mum could not leave as she had three sleeping children in the house, as well as a couple from Manchester who had fled the bombing, so she waited at home. Finally, at six in the morning, she asked a neighbor to come over while she joined Dad at the hospital.

She set out for the hospital in the darkness, not knowing what was going on and desperately worried. As she hurried along the back lane, a black cat darted across her path. Being superstitious, she was alarmed and prayed it was not a bad omen. Alan was conscious when she arrived. The doctor had operated again during the night and had found an abscess. His diagnosis of appendicitis had been wrong.

Alan was very weak. He asked Mum to brush and comb his hair, as if he was expecting to go somewhere special. Mum started to cry as she did so. Then, overcome with tears, she escaped into a little room next to the ward and prayed for Alan to be spared. The sister who had given him the enema came rushing in. She, too, was in tears and she pleaded for Mum's forgiveness. The enema might have made the abscess burst. Peritonitis had set in and without penicillin nothing could be done to treat the infection.

Then Mum was told to come at once. When she got back to Alan's bedside he was gazing up into the far corner of the room. "Look at all those kids up there!" he said with a note of excitement in his voice. Then he was gone. Mum, holding his hand, noticed how warm it felt.

It was November 22, 1943. Alan was 13. He died at nine o'clock - the hour when classes began at the grammar school next door. Mum had seen Alan's classmates, wearing their royal blue caps, passing by the window on their way to school, chattering with one another. Alan's chair would be empty that day.

The doctor had gone home and the matron was left to talk to Mum and Dad. "I was not happy about the first operation," she said, "but of course, ethics had prevented me from telling the doctor so."

My parents took little notice. Nothing mattered now. Alan was dead.

Arrangements had to be made, people had to be contacted. My dear Uncle John came straight from Carlisle to be with us. The minister of our church came to offer his comfort and prayer. Mum and Dad lived through the next few days hardly able to believe what had happened. Alan was too good to die so young. Added to their grief was shock at the suddenness of it.

The day of the funeral, Dad came home, sat down in the chair by the kitchen window and cried. I climbed onto his knee and cried with him, though being so young I couldn't fully comprehend his agony. My heart was filled instead with peace and encouragement. Mum had told me about the heavenly host that had come to meet Alan, and I knew he was with Jesus now. A few days later, I found her standing by the fireplace in the kitchen, crying. I stood on tiptoes and reached up, steadying myself on the mantelpiece. I wanted to comfort her and share the great peace I had in my heart. "Alan is with Jesus in heaven now," I told her gently. "He is very happy there and I know we will see him again."

As Alan entered heaven, it seemed that some of the glory had spilled into my heart. His place in the arms of his Heavenly Father drew me closer, too. After Alan had laid aside his earthly mantle, I found myself clothed with a new spiritual awareness and sensitivity.

"Therefore we also, since we are surrounded by so great a cloud of witnesses…" (Heb. 12:1). These are witnesses such as Abraham, Isaac, Jacob, Joseph, Moses, and many others down through history. I could picture Alan with them, cheering me on to run the race that was set before me.

Even as I had seen the reality of Jesus in Alan's life, I also experienced it in my own. Following my encounter with God in the field, I became aware of all the different kinds of churches. Each had a different name and building, and the people seemed to keep to themselves and their own little groups. Their attitude toward one another was often one of suspicion and criticism. I noticed this attitude was very strong toward the Roman Catholics. In my love for Jesus, I wanted to wear a little cross on a gold chain. Mum told me, "No, you can't. Crosses are a sign of Roman Catholics."

That did not make any sense to me. I thought the cross was a symbol of Jesus' death, not of a denomination. I felt a deep sadness in my heart that the church was so divided and so disunited. Surely, this wasn't God's will for the church. I knew it must grieve His heart, too.

The Lord was beginning to show me His burden, preparing me for the call that He had placed on my life.

Even as I was drawn closer to God, I was also pulled toward the things of Satan. My mother had always been interested in the occult, and this interest deepened after Alan's death. She even attended a séance, hoping to make contact with Alan. I inherited Mum's interest in the supernatural, and she introduced me to astrology, palm reading and teacup reading. Fortune-telling was a regular game at our birthday parties. I was unaware of the danger of dabbling in the occult and the price I would pay for it later. I had the mistaken belief that everything supernatural or psychic was of God and that such practices would bring me closer to Him.

As a child I spent endless hours in a garden shed that I claimed as my own and called "Apple Tree Cottage." I shared it with my friends, my dolls, our pet cat, Mac, and even my brother, David, when we played shops together.

I loved the seasons. In the springtime, Mum would take me into the country where the bluebells spread a fragrant carpet through the woods. It seemed a tragedy to crush them under my feet as I walked. Mum would dig up the primroses and take them home for our garden. The long days of summer were spent outdoors, swimming, roller-skating, and playing in the sand dunes.

Winter was as much fun as summer for the children. It meant countless snowball fights and big fat snowmen. It wasn't so much fun for the grownups. The snow was sometimes deep enough to reach past the kitchen windowsill and cover the hedges, and Dad would have to dig a trench to the street. Our milk turned to ice cream on the doorstep and the water froze in the pipes.

My first move came when Dad decided to move his printing business into a stamp factory on the other side of town. A caretaker's house was provided, and we were better off financially. A few years later, Mum and Dad decided to leave Rhyl and North Wales altogether. At first, they thought of going to Canada where Dad had a cousin. He had another cousin in Australia, and they finally settled on the Great South Land of opportunity instead. We left England on August 12, 1950, sailing from Tilbury docks on the Otranto, a twenty-thousand-ton ocean liner. My eldest brother, John, who had gone to work on a farm when he was 14, decided to stay in Wales until after the harvest, and was to join us in Australia later.

The voyage was an adventure for the family, and particularly for David and me. It was almost too exciting when we caught the tail end of a monsoon in the Indian Ocean. Mum and I were sleeping on deck when it hits, as the cabin was unbearably hot. We woke during the night to find the ship tossing to-and-fro like a cork and great waves breaking against the ship, sending spray across the deck. Mum went below, telling me she would be back. She was overcome with seasickness and when she didn't return, I decided to go down after her. Scared by now, I crawled across the heaving wooden deck making my way to the staircase, and clung desperately to the railing to stop myself from being thrown down the steps. I made it back to the cabin at last. Even when the monsoon had died down, Mum and I still suffered seasickness for a week afterwards. I had never felt so ill in my life.

After weeks of sailing we reached our destination. Mum and Dad chose Sydney, New South Wales, because Dad's cousin who lived there would help us get settled. It was a momentous day when we first stepped onto Australian soil. In His providence, the Lord had brought us to a good land, rugged and beautiful, Australia—or, as the early explorers called it, The Great South Land of the Holy Spirit.

This day would be more significant than I could ever imagine. I would not have to wait too long to discover the unfolding of the next stage of God's plan. Unknown to me, God had a certain young man living in Sydney, Australia He wanted me to meet.

CHAPTER 3

Rejected But Not Forsaken

"Can a woman forget her nursing child and not
have compassion on the son of her womb?
Surely they may forget, yet I will not forget you."
Isaiah 49:15-16

The woman in the hospital delivery room was in the final stages of labor. It wouldn't be long now and Catherine Langstaff would hold her precious baby in her arms. She had waited a long time for her dream to be realized and had prepared for the arrival of the newborn. Tiny nightgowns and booties, blankets and toys were all ready.

Beads of perspiration stood out on her forehead. Her breathing was coming hard and fast. The baby's head was visible now.

"One last push," the doctor said. The pain was so intense, it seemed impossible to her. "Push now!" the doctor said urgently. She mustered up the strength for one more supreme effort and pushed. Then it was over. The baby was in the doctor's hands.

"What is it?" she anxiously blurted out. There was an uncomfortable silence as the doctor hesitated to answer. The silence was broken by the cries of the baby taking its first breath.

"I would rather not say," the doctor cautiously replied. He knew how much she desperately wanted their third child to be a girl.

"Take him away. I don't want him!" she cried out in bitter disappointment.

At this crucial moment, there were no loving arms to welcome this new baby; no kiss on his soft cheek; no whisperings of a mother's love; only rejection.

Catherine and her husband had to keep the baby, of course. Expecting a girl, they had no boy's name picked out. So, when friends and family made suggestions, they put all the names in a hat and drew out the name Alan. They gave him the middle name McGregor, his mother's maiden name, a reminder of his Scottish heritage.

All through his life Alan was reminded that he was supposed to be the girl of the family. It was the story that inevitably came up at family get-togethers. Each time the story was told, people laughed. The effect on Alan was to drive the pain down deeper into his heart and subconscious mind. Consequently, this spirit of rejection clouded his life for 36 years until he was set free on his first trip to America in 1971.

Alan's first toy was a doll. He was the only boy on the block with a doll. He was shy and lacked confidence. His first school photograph shows a little boy hardly able to look at the camera. Later, in his teenage years, he hid all the insecurity behind sarcastic humor, joking and teasing—especially teasing girls.

This lack of confidence and poor self-image was further reinforced as Alan's skin was very much like his mother's. Born in Sterling, Scotland, she had immigrated with her mother and two sisters to Australia. Alan's skin never, ever, went brown, it went pink and freckled and many times he suffered from sunburn. He used to wonder how he could join all the freckles so he could be nicely tanned like his mates and live up to the image of a real Australian man—a bronze Aussie. One time at a Sunday school picnic he escaped from his mother's watchful eye, swam out to a pontoon in the bay in the river, took off his shirt his mother always made him wear and stayed out there all afternoon. The result was severe sunburn and a week in bed recovering.

Alan was born during the Great Depression. At that time, he didn't feel any lack in the home, but later realized that the family had to make do or even go without. For example, they didn't have toilet paper so they had used cut-up newspapers.

The annual vacation was a highlight for Alan. His father worked for the Railway Department, so he obtained free railway passes for their family vacations that took them to places many miles away from Sydney. The family usually went to a seasonal, coastal resort for fun in the sun, especially swimming.

Alan's father, William Langstaff, was born in Yorkshire, England and immigrated to Australia as a young man, eventually enlisting in the armed forces in World War I. He almost went to Gallipoli, but the evacuation of that beachhead took place before he arrived. He ended up serving in France where he was highly decorated, including receiving the Military Medal. Sadly, however, he also received war injuries and had major problems with his hip, resulting in a stiff hip and one leg two inches shorter than the other. After the war he could never run, and walked with a limp.

Alan's two brothers, George and Ken, were eight and six years older than Alan. Both of them excelled at school, graduating from primary school at the top of their respective classes. Alan was expected to do the same, but only ranked second. All of the boys studied at Canterbury Boys' High School.

Ken went into teaching and became a primary school principal. He had a significant influence on Alan in his early years. Being older, he knew more and had more experience in life and in the church than Alan had. Ken was a lay preacher at that time and has now been a leader in the church for well over 50 years.

George was a fine Christian young man admired by all who knew him. He was set for a career as a civil engineer when he contracted cancer in his leg. The doctors amputated his leg, but the cancer had already spread to the lungs. His mother lovingly nursed him at home where he died at the young age of 19. Alan, eight years younger, didn't fully realize what was happening until it was all over and saw the grief that his parents experienced with such a loss.

In spite of the cloud of rejection that overshadowed his birth, Alan had a happy childhood. He nearly died of diphtheria when he was less than 12 months old, and was hospitalized for a month, during which time his parents weren't allowed to visit him. Perhaps it was this event that changed his mother's heart towards him. He felt loved by both his parents as he grew up.

The diphtheria outbreak was but one of the many times when Alan could have died. When he was about four years old, he nearly drowned in a lake. He had panicked and grabbed for his brother when they encountered deep water. About to go down for the third time, he was rescued by a woman, who ran fully clothed into the lake and pulled him to safety. Some years later, at a Sunday school picnic playing chasings with some friends, he ran into a swing and the timber seat split open his head just above his right eye. He contracted blood poisoning. His parents were told that if he didn't improve in the next eighteen hours, he wouldn't make it. In later years, he also had a number of close calls with death. It seemed as though God's hand was on him to preserve him for a future destiny yet to be revealed.

The family belonged to a small Methodist church a little over half a mile's walk from their home in Belmore. They went there because the family did not have a car and it was the closest church.

Sports always attracted Alan. He never excelled in any particular sport but he enjoyed playing football (both rugby league and soccer), cricket and tennis. He also became an ardent supporter of the local rugby league football team, later called the Canterbury Bankstown Bulldogs. The team's home ground in Belmore was within walking distance and he loved to go to watch his team play. His most treasured Christmas present was a brand new cricket bat.

Having struggled through the Great Depression, Alan's parents persuaded him to take a job in the Department of Railways when he graduated from high school. This job provided security for the future as well as a scholarship to study architecture. It may have been secure, but it didn't prove to be very exciting or creative, nor did it allow Alan to develop his full potential. Unknown to him, God had in mind something very different that would later take him in another direction completely. Eventually he left there and took a position at the Sydney University Works Department. This architectural study took seven years. Alan graduated in 1958 and became a registered architect.

At the same time, God was at work in other areas of Alan's life. Increasingly involved in the church, Alan attended church regularly, taught Sunday school, and took part in youth activities. In spite of all that, he was still a nominal Christian.

While at university, he was impressed with the witness of a Salvation Army boy who was also studying architecture. He invited Alan to hear a Scottish preacher, Gavin Hamilton, at some evangelistic meetings. Alan went on that Thursday, steeling himself against any response to the evangelist's appeal. When he went back on the Saturday night, he could not hold back any longer.

In Alan's own words, "I had to respond! He preached the hottest hell-fire sermon I have ever heard. I can still remember the graphic ways he described the fires of hell. I got out of my seat and came down from the balcony. I was in such a state that I staggered down the wrong passage, but eventually found my way to the front of the church and gave my life to Jesus."

Alan realized that being born in a Christian home doesn't make you a Christian any more than being born in a garage makes you a car. He realized he had to be born again and needed a personal relationship with Jesus as Savior and Lord. That decision changed the course of his life and prepared him for his future destiny.

God had other important things planned that also shaped his life—especially a meeting with a young lady from Wales.

CHAPTER 4

God-Directed Choices

*"In all your ways acknowledge Him,
and He shall direct your paths."*
Proverbs 3:6

Sydney, the largest city in Australia, is nestled around one of the most beautiful Harbours in the world. Compared to Rhyl, with its one main street and much smaller population, it was rather overwhelming. Could anyone really belong and feel at home in such a huge place?

We stayed with relatives for a while until Dad found a job as a printer. Then we decided to move into a guesthouse in Strathfield close to the railway station. We ate some of our meals at a little hamburger cafe, and for the rest, Mum bought bread, butter, and other basic food items and kept them in the clothes closet. The weather was so hot compared to the cooler climate of Wales that we felt we were being cooked alive. The heat was like the inside of an oven. Mum used to laugh and say we could cook our bacon and eggs on the concrete path outside.

Living in the guesthouse became so bad that Mum went looking for other accommodations. She found some rooms for rent in a big, old bed and breakfast boarding house in a pleasant part of the residential area. I shared the big-bed sitting room with my parents, while my brother, David, slept on the verandah outside. He was eaten alive by huge mosquitoes until the landlady lent us a mosquito net.

It was good to be just the four of us again. There was a kitchen where Mum could prepare simple meals. A special treat for David and me was finding a cat and family of kittens in an old garage at the back of the house.

Though we were much happier there, we still needed to find a permanent home. So, while Dad was at work and David and I were at school, Mum went out in search of a house. She found a modest but comfortable house in Moorefield Road, Kingsgrove. We signed the papers, but couldn't move in until after Christmas. We celebrated our first Australian Christmas in the boarding house, sitting around the kitchen table and eating baked beans on toast. Our other plans for dinner had fallen through at the last minute.

New Year's Day brought the promise of a better future and my brother, John, to join us. We moved into our new house and settled into a more normal family life. One of the first things my parents did was to find a local church. We had to decide between two churches—an Anglican one on the next hill, and a Methodist church called Moorefields. The latter was convenient, and the Methodist style of worship was comfortably similar to that of the Welsh Congregational Church we had left behind.

The people welcomed us warmly. David and I began Sunday School and soon joined a youth group called the Wesley Guild. This little church became an important part of our family life.

Eventually, David and I also settled into school. My first impressions of school in Australia were not at all pleasant. Most of the children either ignored me or made fun of me and my English accent. Even the teacher was no help. She told me I needn't bother trying to do the work because she would fail me anyway, and she did. Only one girl showed me any kindness. Her name was Jill and hers is the only name I remember.

We reported the unfair treatment to the education department and after sitting for a test I was placed in a junior girls' high school at Marrickville, Sydney. I spent three very happy years there, and I did well at my work. I also became involved in ISCF, Interschool Christian Fellowship, which met in a classroom one hour a week and held weekend retreats during the school year.

My spiritual life deepened and a stronger desire to seek God and fellowship with Him grew inside me. I began to reach out to Him, knowing that there was something more that He wanted to show me of the plan He had for my life. Later I began to teach Sunday School and this also deepened my knowledge of God and my relationship with Him.

Even as I drew closer to God, Satan tried to draw me into the occult, just as he had done when I was a child. A neighbor invited my mother to join a Masonic-type religious organization called the Order of the Eastern Star and suggested that I go to Rainbows, an affiliated group for girls, with her daughter. The order was involved in charity work and social events, and one such social event—a party at a leader's home—introduced me to the party game of "glass moving." The participants would sit around a table with letters of the alphabet on it, an upturned glass in the center. Putting their forefingers lightly on top of the glass, they took turns asking the spirit a question regarding their future. To my amazement, the glass would move and spell out an answer. I was foolish enough to think that I had discovered another way to talk to God. I even shared this experience with my Christian friends at school during a chemistry lesson, using an upturned beaker for a glass.

I found I had a natural gift for communicating with the supernatural. Praise God, there were only these two incidents. He protected me again from the temptation of the enemy and prevented me from getting more involved in the occult.

The Lord was turning my attention to other things, including a fair-haired young man named Alan Langstaff. His family was involved in the church and not surprisingly, Alan and his older brother, Ken, were present at services and youth meetings. I had already noticed this lean boy with bright blue eyes and a cheery grin. I must say that earlier, as a 13-year-old young lady, I had not been favorably impressed. He had a mean sense of humor and gained great satisfaction from teasing the other girls who were older than me. They would blush, giggle and say, "Oh, Alan, you are terrible!" His jokes and constant teasing showed a lack of respect towards young ladies. I would never have tolerated such behavior!

In spite of this, by the time I was 14 and he was 17, my attitude towards Alan had completely changed. I first noticed this when I was sitting next to him on a church pew. He was talking to someone else, and I noticed what a rich deep tone his voice had. I found myself wanting to be where he was. When he hosted church concerts, I even began to find some of his humor amusing. His ready wit and apparent confidence stirred my admiration. I discovered that he had other talents, too. He could play the piano, and he was, to my mind, a really good tennis player.

However, even while I recognized these stirrings within myself, there didn't seem to be any corresponding signs to tell me that Alan even knew I existed. I later discovered he had noticed me when I participated in the Sunday School Anniversary presentations. He didn't tease me as he did the other girls, for which I was very thankful. Perhaps he thought I was too young. I didn't feel too young, though, nor did I look 14. People always thought me to be closer to 18.

My affection for him increased and was typical of the saying "love is blind." Somehow all the things I had previously disliked about him almost disappeared. I began to pray about our friendship and I became convinced that Alan was to be my future husband. I would often draw aside the curtains at night and kneel in the moonlight beside my bed.

I was filled with wonder as I realized God was setting me apart for Alan and the role I would fill as his life partner. "Make me worthy to be Alan's wife," I prayed, believing God had chosen us for each other, not just for marriage, but we were called together to fulfill our future destiny. My prayers were soon answered as, in a natural way, Alan began to notice me and to care about me, too.

Over the next few years, our relationship deepened and we found ourselves organizing our lives so that we could spend more time together. Alan had already graduated from high school and was studying architecture. In 1954, the year following his life-changing experience at the evangelistic meeting, God began to move in our church youth group as well. Quite a number of us became on fire for the Lord through the influence of an American ministry group called "The Musical Messengers." We were ready to take the world for Jesus, no matter what. Our parents and our minister were a little concerned that we were getting carried away. The minister called us together to tell us so and threw a bucket of cold water on all our zeal and enthusiasm.

Alan went on with his architectural studies, and I went to Fort Street Girls' High School. We saw each other every day as we both took the same train into the city. When I finished school, I got a job in the city as a textile artist and attended night classes at East Sydney Technical College in textile design and coloring.

During the next three years I discovered how the "other half" lived. I met so many people who didn't know Jesus. Sometimes I was able to witness for Him, and sometimes I failed miserably. I lived in two different worlds—the world of work and the world of home and church. I knew I didn't belong in the world's lifestyle, nor did I want to.

The Lord made it easy for Alan and me to spend time together. Our offices were within easy walking distance in the city, so we were able to travel into the city together and meet for lunch. We ate our lunch in Hyde Park, among the flowers and fountains and well-kept lawns. It was an oasis in the middle of all the rush and bustle of the city.

It seemed natural for us to talk about marriage, a house and a future together. I didn't even consider a future without Alan in it. We were so young and immature that we thought we had the answer to everything. My parents were concerned that their only daughter, and so young, too, was becoming seriously involved in romance and talking of marriage. There were some conflicts, but realizing we had known each other for six years and were not interested in anyone else, they gave their approval. Mum always thought I had wasted my education, not going to teachers college or university, but I felt I had found my vocation—as Alan's wife. Until that time came, I continued to work as an artist.

When I was 19, Alan and I bought a block of land—virgin bush on the outskirts of Sydney—where we were going to build our dream house. Alan would design it, of course! On my 19th birthday, Alan and I drove out to our land. He placed a diamond ring on the third finger of my left hand. Engaged at last! We returned home to celebrate with the family. The months ahead were filled with excitement and anticipation as we planned for our wedding day.

THE CALL

Chapter 5
Challenges and Changes

Chapter 6
Valley of Trouble

Chapter 7
The Call of Abraham

CHAPTER 5

Challenges and Changes

"Launch out into the deep
and let down your nets for a catch."
Luke 5:4

"Unless the Lord build the house, they labor in vain who build it," (Psa. 127:1). These prophetic words were inscribed on the front page of the Bible given to Alan and me on our wedding day by the young minister who married us. We were married in Moorefields Methodist Church on November 29, 1958. Alan was almost 24 and I had just turned 20. The old church overflowed with friends and relatives who had come to share our joy. Alan, an architect by profession, had a great deal of knowledge about building, but we both had much to learn about building a marriage and family.

Our first building project, with help from friends and family, was a 20-by-10 foot garage on our block of land. We would live there until our house was completed. Our 12 months in the garage were special ones. We had each other and we were very happy, in spite of the inconveniences. Our only plumbing was one faucet that came through the wall. We washed everything, including ourselves, in a basin beneath it, and emptied the dirty water outside. Once or twice a week, we went home to our mothers for showers and laundry, both of us astride Alan's 300-pound Heinkel motor scooter with a big bundle of washing tied on the back. It was a funny sight.

We furnished our garage with an old table and chairs, a cupboard or two, and two single beds pushed together. Our lifestyle was primitive, but fun! There was only one other house nearby, so it was an isolated place to live. I didn't mind the solitude. My cattle dog, Scottie, gave me plenty of company and protection in Alan's absence. He took his responsibility so seriously that, on a number of occasions, he tried to protect me from Alan, too.

I left my work in the city and enjoyed life at home. While Alan was at work, I began to develop our land, digging and carrying wheelbarrow loads of soil to fill new garden beds. Later, when the house was built, I did a lot of the painting. I also worked part-time in my parents' grocery store.

We began attending a Methodist Church nearby. Breaking ties with his family, friends and Moorefields Church, proved to be a growth experience for Alan. He found himself gaining more self-confidence during our first year of marriage than in any previous year. He was thrust into many responsibilities in the local church as well as at home. Then, three years later, came the new responsibility of fatherhood.

We decided to start a family after we were settled in the house. Our first baby was soon on the way. For the first three months of my pregnancy, I was ill with morning sickness—misnamed in my case, because I was sick day and night. The one advantage was that I lost surplus weight. I grew so slim that even later in my pregnancy, it was difficult to tell that I was carrying a baby.

Our dear little baby was born on June 20, 1961. When she was first placed beside me, I thought she looked just like a little cherub, with her big blue eyes, delicate skin and rosebud mouth. We called her Beth. I had always said that my first little girl would be called Beth. Our happiness increased with the delight of a new baby to love and care for—until she was about twelve months old.

Almost overnight, our happiness was shattered. Beth became asthmatic. We struggled to adjust to the fact. I didn't even know what asthma was at first. We took her to doctors and read books in a desperate effort to find some sort of cure or even temporary relief. It didn't help us. We discovered that Beth had inherited asthma from Alan's family. Both Alan and his brother, Ken, had had it.

We began to discover what triggered her asthma—things she inhaled and things she ate. Milk was a major culprit. It had always been difficult for her to digest, and now we knew why. She had a serious allergy, not only to milk, but also to nearly all proteins.

Beth was a chronic asthmatic, and even daily medication couldn't prevent bad asthma attacks. Severe attacks were a nightmare. The only relief consisted in wheeling Beth's stroller around the house, Alan and I alternating half-hour shifts all night and into the next day, until the attack subsided. Often, we had to call the doctor to give her an injection or take her to the hospital for treatment.

Finally, I decided to put Beth on a strict diet, supplemented with vitamins. This, together with physiotherapy over a period of years, reduced the attacks. Even then, every cold she caught would develop into a bad asthma attack, bronchitis, or even pneumonia.

Despite asthma and the confinement it brought, Beth had an adventurous love of life and the outdoors. She also developed a keen imagination and passion for reading. What she wasn't able to do physically, she made up for in imaginary games. And even though she was absent from school a great deal, she still did very well in her studies.

Beth's arrival and then her asthma brought dramatic changes to our home life. At the same time, a change in the direction of Alan's career caused equally dramatic results.

Alan had been almost 20 when God first began challenging him about the ministry. He heard Alan Walker, a leading Australian Methodist minister preach at a youth convention in 1955, and watched young men step forward and commit themselves to full-time ministry. Alan walked out of the auditorium thinking that was the last thing in the world he wanted to do. Later, he realized that one of the reasons he didn't want to be a minister was that he had never met or heard a pastor who excited him in any way.

That changed later that year on one Sunday night after church when he picked up and read a Reader's Digest condensed version of the book *A Man Called Peter* by Catherine Marshall. The book was the story of a young Scottish immigrant, called of God into the ministry, who eventually became the chaplain of the U.S. Senate. Through this and other confirming experiences, Alan knew that God was giving him a challenge. He was being called to the ministry.

The news wasn't a surprise to me; I had already sensed that one day I would be a pastor's wife. I felt an inner witness, a stirring of the strong feeling of destiny within me. I believed we were called of God together. I knew that Alan was not going to be a typical minister, even though Alan had no intention of being anything special. God had something different planned for him.

Before we were married, Alan had begun to do a little preaching, and several people asked him if he had ever considered going into the ministry. Even his boss in the architecture office commented, "One day you're going to end up with your collar back to front." Alan knew for sure that God wanted him to be a minister, but he didn't know what to do about it. It was sobering to realize that he might have to give up university and his architectural career. Perhaps he would even have to put aside the desire to get married, build his own house and establish a family.

It had come to a climax one day while we were sitting in the car at the local shopping center. Alan had to lay it all on the altar. We decided to give God the first choice in our lives—not our will, but His will.

For Alan, it was the same kind of experience that Abraham had when God asked him to sacrifice Isaac. After he had been willing to lay down his hopes and dreams for the future, God had given them back. God clearly indicated that we were to get married, build our house, and that Alan was to finish his architectural course. At a later time, he would go into ministry.

In January 1960, a new minister came to Padstow Methodist Church. Lacking advanced education, Colin Orton had been ordained because of his faithful work in home missions in the outback of Queensland. But he knew the Lord, and he knew the foundation of scripture as the Word of God.

Alan had not been sure of that foundation; liberal Methodist theology had sown doubts. But Colin Orton gave him a book to read, Dr. James Packer's *Fundamentalism and the Word of God*, which gave Alan the assurance that God's Word was trustworthy and true. Strangely enough, Alan never finished reading the book. When he came to the chapter about Jesus and the scriptures and realized that Jesus never repudiated anything in the Old Testament and even affirmed controversial events such as Jonah and the whale, it was the turning point for Alan. He decided that if it was good enough for Jesus, it was good enough for him.

From that time onward it was settled once and for all. The Bible was to be the basis of what he believed, taught and sought to live. He accepted it as true and trustworthy, and it became the foundation of his life. That foundation was strengthened by other books such as Catherine Marshall's *Beyond Ourselves* and a study booklet called *Victorious Christian Living*.

Alan, however, had become comfortable as an architect. He enjoyed his work at the university and still made no definite plans for the ministry. It wasn't until Colin Orton stood on our front doorstep one day in 1961 and said, "Hadn't you better make up your mind what God has called you to be—an architect or a minister—and get on with it?"

Alan was convicted that it was time to enter the Methodist ministry. He candidated in 1962 and began training in 1963. For the next five years, he worked as a student pastor in the Punchbowl Greenacre circuit. Alan quickly learned the old adage, "Ashes to ashes and dust to dust, what the Pastor won't do the assistant must." So he did a bit of everything, even teaching religious instruction in the public schools, with classes from kindergarten right through to senior high. He was involved with the youth and led Vacation Bible Schools and, as was typical of that era, was expected to visit as many people as possible in their homes. And, of course, he would preach every Sunday, usually twice in the morning and once at night.

It was a very satisfying time for him. Not only did he enjoy his classes at seminary, even though he disagreed with his liberal professors many times, but he also had the practical opportunity of being involved in pastoral ministry. Although I was able to go to church services and lead the women's meetings once a month, I became a little frustrated. I felt confined to home and the care of Beth. *If only I could be more involved in ministry with Alan*, I thought. One day I was taking the usual load of washing down the garden path to the laundry and God spoke directly to my heart. "Your children are your first disciples," He said. I heard His message loud and clear. My most important ministry at that time was right in my own home.

Alan also had the experience of serving under four different senior pastors in five years, all of them different in personality and the way they went about ministry. He always remembered the first time he sat down with his first senior pastor and being told, "If we are going to work together then there must be loyalty between us." It was a piece of advice that helped Alan to navigate through the years with senior pastors with whom he did not see eye to eye theologically.

Alan did well in his first year at seminary, so much so that the college staff decided he should pursue a Bachelor of Divinity degree (a post-graduate degree the equivalent of a Master of Divinity Degree in America) through the Melbourne College of Divinity. However, Alan faced one hurdle. Although he had studied Architecture at the University of New South Wales, he had only received a diploma in Architecture, sufficient to qualify as a member of the Royal Australian Institute of Architects.

In 1964 it was decided that he should go back to the same university and complete what was termed a conversion course to convert the architecture diploma into a bachelor's degree.

Normally, this was attempted over a two-year period of part-time study, but since Alan wanted to pursue his theological education as quickly as possible, he sought and received permission to do the course in one year, the first person at that time allowed to do so.

His coursework involved a number of subjects including philosophy—a subject that Alan approached with some reservations, as he thought it might undermine his faith. On the contrary, he came to the conclusion that it was all built on human presuppositions and that it didn't threaten his faith at all.

The main task however, was to present a major thesis and he chose the subject "The Theological Basis of Methodist Church Architecture," believing that would be of benefit for him, and maybe others, in the ministry. The procedure was to work under a professor and, having received approval for your topic, present an outline of the projected study and then move ahead in your research.

Halfway through the year, Alan presented his preliminary work to the professor. He was not impressed. Figuratively speaking, he ripped up his report and virtually said he had better start again. It was for Alan a devastating moment. Discouraged, he told himself that he had been foolish to try to do the two-year course in only one year on top of all his parish duties and family responsibilities, and that he should complete the other subjects and concentrate on the thesis in the following year.

He would have done that, except that I strongly exhorted him to try again. Or as Alan put it many years later, "She gave me a good kick in the pants to get me out of my pity party."

"What have you got to lose if you give it another try? All that will happen is you will have to do it next year anyway," I told him. "Maybe you could do it this year after all."

Something was sparked in Alan and he re-entered the fray with renewed zeal and vision and with what must have been a touch of divine inspiration. He worked hard, studied long, and finally presented the thesis for examination in addition to completing the other subjects. The Christian secretary at his old architectural office typed the thesis on what was then the new IBM electric typewriter.

As a reward for his efforts, Alan received the highest marks he ever received at university. In all but one subject he received "Distinctions" and for his thesis he received a "High Distinction," the highest possible grade that could be given.

This achievement had a major positive effect on Alan's self-image and confidence, bearing in mind the lack of a positive self-image that went back to the rejection he had experienced at birth. It also showed him that he was capable of far more than he thought he could do. Out of it came an understanding of the importance of zeal and passion in pursuing God-given goals. It also demonstrated for him the great contribution and value of having me as his wife, for without my encouragement he would have given up.

So in 1965, in his third year as a student pastor, Alan went on to begin his Bachelor of Divinity studies, all of which he loved, except for Hebrew and Greek, as he never had a gift for biblical languages. However, he managed to pass these language examinations and went on to successfully complete his graduate degree.

Everything seemed almost idyllic. We enjoyed the work at the church and our quiet home. Little Beth brought us great joy and delight, but a nagging feeling began to rise within us. Little did we know that life was about to bring another dramatic change. There was something missing. Could it be God wanted us to have another child?

CHAPTER 6

Valley of Trouble

"Weeping may endure for a night,
but joy comes in the morning."
Psalm 30:5

Everyone told me that the second time would be easier. I had been so sick during my first pregnancy and Beth had been so ill, I was apprehensive about having more children. Now, however, we were convinced that we were to have another baby, and God gave me fresh courage.

So, I was surprised to recognize the familiar feeling of nausea. Surprise gave way to dismay as a repeat performance of my first pregnancy began. I waited for the sickness to pass, but it became worse. I couldn't keep any food down and couldn't handle even a glass of water. As I became too weak and sick to function, Alan had to take over most household duties. The smell of cooking was unbearable, let alone the thought of eating it. Each night I slept with a bowl next to my pillow.

My doctor gave me pills to settle the sickness, but they only made me feel more dull and lifeless. He was concerned about dehydration, so he advised a week's stay in the hospital.

As soon as I was admitted, they began injections. My doctor came around later, and, amazed, found me wide-awake. The massive dose of injected tranquilizers should have knocked me out. They continued the treatment, and the nausea subsided slightly. I picked at my food and tried to drink lots of fluids.

The doctors released me from the hospital, reassuring me that the sickness would soon pass. I felt too weak to go home, so I went to my mother's for a week. I took the pills that were supposed to settle my stomach, but the sickness persisted. I began to eat a little. I craved pears, so Dad searched the shops to find them.

Alan and Beth, meanwhile, were staying with Alan's mother and father. In answer to my questions, Alan assured me Beth was all right. I wasn't prepared for her condition when she and Alan came to take me home from my mother's. When Alan brought Beth into Mum and Dad's living room, I was shocked. My heart ached at the sight of her pale, drawn little face. She had obviously lost a lot of weight. A perpetual nervous cough had developed. My absence had left her frightened and terribly insecure.

When Mum took Beth through to the back of the house, I turned to face Alan, saying, "Why didn't you tell me what was going on? I would have come home, even if I was sick."

We returned home to try and pick up the pieces. Beth recovered slowly. I continued to be sick 24 hours a day. Helpless and miserable, I watched Alan run off his feet trying to cope with his duties at church as well as looking after his wife, daughter and home. Mum was no longer there to help. She and Dad had just bought a corner shop on the other side of the city and that took most of their time. Alan had to manage on his own.

Hours dragged into days, days into weeks, and weeks into months. The only comfort was that I couldn't go on being sick forever. Sooner or later, it had to stop. And it did eventually, at the end of the fourth month. The doctor told me I could discontinue the pills, but now I faced a new problem—I was addicted to them.

Without them, I was an emotional wreck and unable to sleep. The doctor was puzzled as the pills were supposed to be harmless, non-habit forming tranquilizers. They hadn't affected any of his other patients this way. He could only suggest to continue taking them until the baby was born. I was horrified to learn that I was dependent on the little white sugarcoated pills. If I had known they were tranquilizers and that they would have such an effect, I would have refused to take them.

I had been lethargic and dull while taking them, but now I plunged into depression as well. What if I was addicted forever? I tried to comfort myself that everything would return to normal when the baby was born. Meanwhile, I grew stronger. With Alan's help, I tried to do as many chores as possible. Now that I was not vomiting constantly, I could spend more time with Beth, particularly during the night when she was sick with asthma.

We visited our parents regularly. My mother told us about a family who lived across the road from the shop. The wife told Mum all her problems when she came for groceries; the main one being her non-Christian husband, who was dying of cancer. His Catholic wife was afraid that his soul would go to hell. Mum mentioned to her that Alan was a minister and asked if we could help.

As the weeks of my pregnancy went by, we made frequent visits to share and pray with this couple. Alan spent hours talking to the husband, while I shared with Alice, who had deep needs of her own. Her husband accepted Christ just before he died, but the grief that followed his death sent Alice into deep depression. It became clear that more was wrong in this troubled home than grief. Alice had been involved in the occult and now she was playing with a Ouija board, talking to evil spirits. Her eldest son, a Satan worshipper, was up to the hilt in crime. Another son was a Christian who couldn't break free of homosexuality. Of the two sons still at home, one was an asthmatic and the other was hyperactive.

Weird things began to occur. Alice started to hear voices. She would call me at all hours of the day and night, overcome with fear, and I would pray with her over the phone. I was struggling with my own fears at the time, so I felt like the blind trying to lead the blind. Miraculously, I was able to give her some strength and comfort, even when I had none myself.

We were too inexperienced to deal with the real problem—Alice was demon possessed. We had been thrown into the deep end of spiritual warfare, unable to swim. We had no idea how to fight that kind of battle, let alone how to protect ourselves. My mind became a target for Satan's oppression.

Obsessional fears took control and bombarded me unmercifully. Noises suddenly began to annoy me. We lived under the major flight path to Sydney airport, and I began to dread the sound of the big jets flying overhead. Every time one went over, my mind felt as if it was in a vice, even though I tried counteracting it by praising the Lord. But, I wasn't harassed only by the planes. The noise of ticking clocks, motors, breaking waves, birds, crickets and bugs all made life unbearable. The only peace was sleep.

Satan harassed my eyes as well as my ears. At first, it was an unusual sensitivity to bright turquoise. That particular color leapt out at me. The sight of it went through me like a knife. I had to put vases and clothing away because I couldn't bear to be in the same room with them. Other bright colors began to have the same effect. I couldn't bear to wear them. If my dress had a bold pattern, I would be uncomfortable until I changed it for a plain one. I wished I could just wear a beige or gray uniform to get peace of mind.

I found little relief or comfort in prayer. God seemed so far away. I would sit in the living room listening to George Beverly Shea singing "His eye is on the sparrow and I know He cares for me." In my mind I could see myself hanging on to God by a single thread. There seemed no way out of the overwhelming darkness and oppression. Our Senior Pastor and his wife came to see us and prayed for God's help, but didn't know what else to do.

Special days like Christmas or birthdays were especially hard. The happier I was supposed to be, the more miserable I became. Even a picnic was a nightmare. We went to one church picnic at a park overlooking a beach. I looked down the cliff to the waves crashing on the rocks and felt overwhelmed with hopelessness. I thought of others who must have felt as I did and found a way to end it.

I had an overwhelming desire to die. I felt I had nothing to live for, and I could only think of wanting it all to end. I forced myself to keep busy, but my tiredness only made me more miserable. Even the garden that we had created from virgin bush held no relief or joy now. I stared down at the stones on the path that crunched under my feet and wished I could die. My conscience wouldn't allow suicide. So, I would sit in the car on the side of a busy road and pray for a truck to come hurtling along and finish me off.

In February, I developed toxemia and the doctor put me back in the hospital. Two weeks later, he decided to induce the baby. He felt it would be wiser than waiting another three or four weeks. I was relieved that this difficult time would soon be over.

On March 2, 1967, I gave birth to our second baby girl. She was a healthy, happy baby, completely unaffected by the entire trauma, and her coming was like a comforting balm to me. We decided to call her Joy. It seemed the right name. She brought joy in the midst of trial and she was a promise of joy for the future. It was as if the Lord was saying, "You shall call her Joy because she shall bring you joy and blessing. You will be brought from sorrow into joy."

This was reassuring, but the trial was far from over.

CHAPTER 7

The Call of Abraham

"By faith Abraham obeyed . . . and he went out,
not knowing where he was going."
Hebrews 11:8

Even while I had been upstairs in the maternity ward, Alan was downstairs in the emergency room with Beth while she received medication and oxygen for a severe asthma attack. In the months after Joy's birth, we had to make frequent visits to the hospital, as Beth had chronic asthma again day and night.

I was still depressed and addicted to the tranquilizers. Alan was still trying to manage the home, his theological studies, and his duties at church. He was at the point of collapse, overwhelmed by the pressure of circumstances, and unable to fully cope. He felt as though he was on the edge of a bottomless pit and was about to fall in.

In the midst of all this stress, he was attending a clergy training course at a psychiatric hospital. On the final day of class he happened to sneeze and his back went out. He doubled over in agony, finding it difficult to straighten up again. Several years earlier he had strained the muscles in his back while trying to move a large slab of concrete in our backyard.

But with the stress in his life now, this time it only took a sneeze.

Throughout the day his back became progressively worse, so they put him on a bed in the hospital and gave him some medication, which didn't help him very much. The problem was how to get him home, as he couldn't get into the small car he was driving at the time. Eventually, a Baptist minister who was attending the course with Alan and had a station wagon, offered to drive him home.

They laid Alan out in the back of the station wagon. There he lay helpless, dressed in his best suit, briefcase beside him, outside the admission center to the psychiatric hospital. Passers-by saw him lying there and stared at him curiously, thinking "I wonder what's wrong with him?"

That night he was in excruciating pain and our own doctor came and gave him a shot of morphine. Feeling euphoric, Alan said he could now understand how people could get hooked on drugs.

Somehow, we made it through the winter of 1967. But by October, with no relief in sight, we reached our desperation point. We couldn't go on any longer. The Methodist Annual Conference was due to meet in October, and Alan was up for appointment as a two-year probationary minister. The Conference would probably send us to a country church. The thought of pastoring any new church was more than we could bear. Alan decided the best thing to do was apply for a year's rest and try to get our lives in order.

He attended the conference meetings and tried to concentrate on the affairs in question. But he could only wonder if he would be given permission to step down for a year's rest. Finally, appointments came up on the agenda and he heard his name read out. "Alan Langstaff—no appointment—given permission to stand down for one year due to extenuating circumstances."

With a sigh of relief, he hurried home to tell me the good news. He arrived home at six. I was in the kitchen, just about to serve dinner, when he came in and announced, "Well, they've granted us a year's rest."

"That's good," I said, trying to put up a brave front.

Then I paused, a saucepan in one hand and a serving spoon in the other, and stared down at the bright yellow counter with the plates on it. A silence spread over me. It was broken by the penetrating, monotonous whistle of a bird somewhere in the bush. The sound seared my mind like a red-hot knife. With it came fear. Why didn't Alan's news give me any relief or peace?

The following week was a long, torturous nightmare. My fears and depression increased. Every noise leapt out of the silence to deal me another blow, especially the bird whistle with its monotonous regularity.

I woke up with a start in the middle of the night. There was no noise, only silence—deathly and uncanny silence. Something tangible—to be felt, not heard. I listened for the slightest sound. Nothing. The silence itself was screaming at me. I woke Alan to pray for me and finally slept.

The next morning was Sunday. The unrest of the previous night hampered us as we tried to have breakfast, feed the baby, and dress the children. We were going to be late for church.

It had occurred to Alan and me that perhaps God was trying to say something to us. Taking a year's rest was the logical thing to do, but since Alan had brought the news of permission granted, we had gone through hell. We stood in the bedroom and prayed, "Lord, perhaps a year's rest isn't the right thing. We haven't gained any release at all. There certainly hasn't been any rest. Maybe You are trying to tell us that You don't want us to take a rest at all, but You want us to take an appointment. Please show us what Your will is. Do we go or stay?"

God would have to answer that very day for us to reverse our decision. The Methodist Conference had almost finished its business for the year.

That morning, we attended our little church that was in the process of closing down and merging with another nearby church. It was a special service and a guest speaker had been invited. By the time we arrived, the only seats left were up in the front, right underneath the pulpit, and the preacher was about to read the Old Testament lesson.

Later in the service he began his sermon with the arresting words, "Go and take little with you." He told the story of God speaking to Abraham, calling him to leave his home and family and set out for a land that God would show him. We nudged elbows and glanced at one another excitedly. This was God's answer to our dilemma. He wanted us to leave our home and take an appointment. There wasn't a shadow of doubt about that.

As the sermon progressed, it was as though the preacher had received a dossier on our specific circumstances and had prepared the sermon just for us. It was clear God was personally speaking to us through this message. He knew the story of Abraham would become the inspiration for our walk of faith and that Hebrews 11:8, *"And he (Abraham) went out, not knowing where he was going,"* would become the pattern for our life. This was the first time we had received such dramatic guidance.

Now, not a moment could be lost. That afternoon we sought out the principal of the Theological College and explained what had happened. He looked at us calmly, and said, "If that is what God wants you to do, we'll accept that." He took our request to the conference the next day, and our names were put back on the appointment sheet for placement in a church the following January. We had been added to the list just in time.

They decided to send us to Bexley, a Sydney suburb only a few miles away from where we were living, not out to the country, as was the usual practice with probationers.

Even though we were obedient to the Lord's will, there was still no relief from the oppression. But there was no turning back now. We hoped that in moving from Padstow to Bexley we would move from the bondage of Egypt to the Promised Land of Canaan.

We arranged to rent our house to a Christian couple and began the mammoth task of packing. After living in our house for nine years, we had accumulated a great deal. At this point, we had forgotten the phrase, "Take little with you."

Not only did we have to face decisions about household goods, but I loved our house and garden. They were a part of us. Alan and I had toiled countless hours together, laying paths, planting and landscaping. It was hard for me to realize that we would have to leave this little piece of earth that had become so dear.

I thought perhaps I could take a few mementos with me, so I took a bucket and scissors and walked rather wistfully round the garden to take cuttings from the willow tree, the creeper with the pretty blue flowers, and a few other favorites. I put them in water in the laundry, ready for the garden at Bexley.

But I started to get an uneasy feeling as I continued packing. Surely it is all right to take a few cuttings, I reasoned. Then why did I feel so bad?

God whispered His answer to my heart, "This garden is precious to you, but I want you to leave it behind, every bit of it. There is to be no looking back for you, only forward."

My home and garden could easily have become an idol. I know if I tried to hang onto them in any way, I would not be able to wholly follow the Lord. Before we left, I gave every last cutting away. Later, I was delighted to find not one but four willow trees in the new garden.

Now it was time to go. The final trip was made. We paused for a moment on the threshold to commit the use of the house to God. There were no tears. We knew that God was closing the door on a chapter of our lives. I never returned to that house until the summer of 1989, over 20 years later, and I never desired to.

We went forth with anticipation. God had called us to step out in faith into an unknown future to fulfill our destiny in Him. We moved into the parsonage provided for us by the West Bexley Church, only a few doors away from the church. We had taken this step of faith and obedience instead of taking a year's rest, but to our horror, things grew worse. We went from the frying pan into the fire.

I cried out to God continually with no permanent answer forthcoming. Again and again I would go to Alan and he would pray for me, claiming the blood of Jesus on my mind and rebuking the devil as best he knew how. For a short time the enemy's siege would ease, only to return with an increasing number of fiery darts and mental torment. I came to the end of myself.

It amazed me that even in the midst of this period I could leave the house every Monday, depressed, go to lead a ladies Bible study where the Lord's anointing was obviously present, and return home to my depressed state again. I would tell the ladies, "I know there is something more, more power to live victoriously, and when I find it I'll let you know."

But the opposition of the enemy, my depression, and the continual barrage of fears were more than I could bear. There didn't seem to be an answer to my desperate situation.

A doctor had exchanged the little white pills I was addicted to for different ones, thinking this would help me to break the addiction. Over a period of months, with God's help and much prayer, I cut down on the tranquilizers. I would cut one of the little shiny blue pills in half, reducing the dosage each month until finally I was on half a pill each day. Then, at last, I was free of them altogether.

One day when I couldn't stand it any more, I decided if God didn't bring an answer in the next month I would go to a psychiatrist (for me a last resort) even though I doubted he would have an answer. So Alan and I stood together in the hallway of the parsonage and agreed together for God to intervene and send help in the next month. The days and weeks slowly went by with still no answer, no sign of rescue. Then, right at the end of the month, a young man at church loaned Alan a book to read. Alan didn't have time to do so, but as he was supposed to meet and talk about it, he asked me to read it instead. The book was called *They Speak With Other Tongues* by John Sherrill.

It was Sunday afternoon when I began reading. Leaving the dirty dishes in the sink, I put Beth and Joy in the swimming pool to play, settled in a deck chair on the patio overlooking the pool, and began the task of reading. I would never get through it in time for tonight. Normally, I took days to read a book. In no way was I a fast reader.

Becoming engrossed in the book, I read page after page and discovered it was talking about the "something more" I had been looking for, but hadn't known what it was. The book explained it all very clearly. I came to the obvious conclusion that I needed the Baptism in the Holy Spirit to give me the power I desperately needed. There was an excitement in me I had never experienced before and a light of hope was lit in my heart. I couldn't put the book down.

I was sure by now that Beth and Joy had been in the water so long they would have wrinkled skin on their fingers, yet they seemed happy enough. Then at the back of my mind I remembered the pile of dirty dishes in the kitchen. I simply had to clean up by six. That was when everyone was due to arrive to discuss this book. No! The dishes could wait. I had to read.

It seemed like hours had passed before, miracle of miracles, I actually finished the book. I hurried into the kitchen and couldn't believe my eyes when I anxiously looked at the clock. The small hand and the large hand were both at two. That meant it was ten minutes past two. It must have stopped. That had to be the explanation. I had gone out to read at two o'clock, only ten minutes earlier. Checking the other clocks in the house I was astonished to find that they all had the same time. The clock hadn't stopped. Time had somehow stood still. I knew that this was God's intervention in answer to our desperate prayer. He had chosen a very remarkable way to do so. Somehow, very soon, I would experience the Baptism in the Holy Spirit.

Later that week I picked up a little blue and white tract written by Dr. Bill Bright. On the front page it asked the question, "Have you made the wonderful discovery of the

Spirit-filled life?" It outlined simple steps on how to received the Spirit with a picture of a train; the engine (fact), the tender car (faith), and last of all to follow, the carriages (feelings). So, I prayed a simple prayer that day sitting in my living room. Joy was having a sleep, Beth was at school, and Alan was out. I asked God to baptize me in His Holy Spirit and waited.

I expected something to happen as they had described in John Sherrill's book, but nothing seemed to happen. I even tried waggling my tongue thinking I would speak in tongues any minute—still nothing. The only sound was the buzzing of a fly on the windowpane. I felt a bit disappointed. *Oh well,* I thought, *I've tried.*

I thought nothing had happened, but from that time on I noticed three major changes that began to take place in my life. First, I began to be filled with the love of God for people in a new way. Second, the word of God came alive and leapt off the pages of my Bible. Finally, I began to experience some of the gifts of the Spirit, including words of knowledge and prophetic insight. The release to speak in tongues would not happen until later. At the time, perhaps it was just as well. In contrast to my enthusiasm and hunger for more of the Spirit, Alan was hesitant and skeptical of the Modern-Day Pentecostal movement and did not want to get involved.

When it came time for the 1968 Billy Graham Crusade in Sydney, Alan jumped in with both feet, and we both volunteered as counselors. It was the first time I had been involved in something that would touch a city and change thousands of lives. I sat in the counselors training sessions and saw hundreds of Christians from so many denominations laying aside their differences to come together in unity for one common cause. This stirred something deep in my spirit.

"Unity—isn't that what God wants?" I mused. "Think what could be accomplished if the church was united and not divided. Didn't Jesus pray that we would be one?"

I was convinced that not only did God have something more for me, personally, but also for the whole Body of Christ.

THE PREPARATION

CHAPTER 8

Deliverance From Evil

"For we do not wrestle against flesh and blood,
but against principalities, against powers . . ."
Ephesians 6:12

The year 1968 turned out to be a year of rapid spiritual growth for Beth, as well as for me. In April, Beth went forward at the Billy Graham Crusade to make a decision for Jesus. Her born-again experience affected every area of her life, but still her asthma persisted. By June, she was so sick and frail that Alan and I, at the point of despair, knelt together at the sofa in the living room and handed Beth over to the Lord to live or die.

As we prayed a prayer of relinquishment, I saw in my mind a picture of us handing Beth's limp form into the extended arms of Jesus. "She is Yours, Lord," I said, "to do with as You will. She is no longer ours."

A profound peace followed our time of prayer. And, although she knew nothing of our prayer, for a month afterwards Beth was completely free of asthma. God was showing us that He had heard our prayers and received our offering.

We thought she had been healed and we were puzzled when the asthma returned in full force. I had been reading books on healing and attended several meetings of the Order of St. Luke, a healing ministry that taught on healing and prayed for the sick. I had begun to believe that God wanted to heal people. We had Beth prayed for with laying-on of hands, but the severe asthma persisted.

There was so much I didn't understand. During the night I was often aware of a heavy, dark presence around her bed. I would usually awake afraid, feeling the same presence. One night, a supernatural light appeared in the hallway, grew brighter, and then disappeared.

Our house wasn't the only one with odd visitors. We were still regularly counseling Alice, the demon-possessed woman. She was aware of cold presences in her house that sent ornaments flying off the wall and crashing onto the floor across the room. Unexplained voices harassed her and she was almost always in a state of fear and terror.

Alice needed help desperately, and so did we. Toward the end of 1968, we realized we couldn't go on like this. We didn't know what to do and we cried out to the Lord for help. I knew the Order of St. Luke had a group of intercessors who prayed more extensively for individuals, so I contacted the leader of the group and explained our predicament. She wouldn't ask the ladies to pray for Alice in case they, too, came under attack from Satan. She did, however, give us the names of two ministers who knew how to deal with demon possession. One, Noel Gibson, the director of a leading evangelistic ministry, had great spiritual authority. We called and asked for help and they agreed to meet Alan at Alice's house. When they heard that I had been involved in the occult, they advised me not to go. From the description of my condition, they thought I was demon-possessed as well.

Alan, for the first time in his life, found himself watching an exorcism. When the ministers addressed the demons, several voices—none of them belonging to Alice—answered. The multiple male voices shrieked and screamed as Noel Gibson took authority over Satan in the name of Jesus, commanding them to leave. Watching Alice's face and body contort, Alan felt as though he was watching a wrestling match.

It took three hours of deliverance to drive out all the demons. Noel Gibson later declared that Alice was one of the worst cases of demon possession he had encountered over years of experience in New Zealand and Australia. But, *at the name of Jesus every knee should bow, of those in heaven, and of those on earth," (Phil. 2:10).* Alice saw Satan as a form of light on his knees before the ministers. Jesus is Lord! Hallelujah!

When Noel Gibson felt there was nothing more he could do for Alice, it was time to head for our house. He was anticipating another deliverance session with me. He wasted no time. After a brief explanation, he asked me to kneel and began to pray. I really didn't care what happened, as long as I was set free. I was almost disappointed when he interrupted his prayer.

He said, after a pause, "I have been mistaken. The Lord has just shown me that you are not demon-possessed, but severely harassed and oppressed. The signs can almost be the same."

He finished praying for me against the oppression. Later, he and his wife, Phyl, said, "You know, we think it could be that the enemy is oppressing you, not because of your past but because of your future. The enemy doesn't know everything, but he has wind of how God wants to use you and Alan in the future, and he is trying to prevent it from happening."

For me, however, it was an anti-climax. I knew the battle wasn't over. During the next few days I was overwhelmed by a huge wave of depression. Now, help seemed even further away.

Further contact with Noel and Phyl Gibson did shed light on our situation. They gave us insight and strategies on how to cope with the spiritual warfare. They felt that to the great extent that we were suffering the enemy's attack, so God would use us mightily in the future. The devil knew that we were a threat to his evil plans. Again I was encouraged by the sense of destiny on my life. This enabled me to hold fast to the Lord.

Each time the oppression came on my mind, I would ask Alan to pray for me, and he would take authority over the enemy and claim the blood of Jesus to protect me. This gave temporary relief, but I knew there must be more answers.

Beth spent the last three months of third grade at home. One of her teachers at school had a harsh temper and the tense atmosphere in the classroom left her sick and terrified. The doctor advised us to remove her from school.

Alan, too, came under attack. One day he was walking home from the church, carrying an empty ice cream bucket and a blue plastic spoon. Suddenly he heard a rumbling noise behind him. Without even pausing to glance back, he dropped the bucket and spoon and he felt propelled forward. When he stopped running, he turned and stared with horror. A huge truck had gone through a stop sign at the nearby intersection, crashed into a car, and the two vehicles mounted the footpath and ended up against a low brick wall—exactly at the spot where Alan had been a moment before.

I had been in the back garden when I heard the crash and I immediately began to rebuke the devil, not knowing that Alan was in danger. I hurried around to the front of the house and found Alan, white-faced and shaking.

When the truck was removed we went back to the spot. The tires had left skid marks and huge gouges on the grassy footpath. The blue plastic spoon was flattened on the footpath, shattered in pieces. It was a sober image of what could have happened to Alan if he had paused to look back.

It wasn't until early 1969 that we received new insight. Don Evans, one of our friends in the Methodist ministry, held charismatic prayer meetings in his home and invited us to attend. During the course of the evening, several of the pastors who were present laid hands on Alan and me and prayed for us. I felt a strange sensation in my diaphragm area, like a huge pancake turning over and over and trying to rise up within me.

I didn't understand what was happening, but I believe it was the Holy Spirit. Afterwards, a wise, elderly man, Pastor Evans from Brisbane, asked me if I had ever been involved in the occult. I explained my childhood involvement, but was quick to tell him that it was my mother who had introduced me to the occult. That didn't matter, he informed me; I still needed to confess my sin and ask forgiveness. Until I did, Satan would have the grounds to harass and oppress me.

I listened, but inwardly I was struggling with the blame. At home the next day, Alan led me in a prayer of repentance. I told him I would say the prayer in faith, but in my heart I still felt it wasn't my fault. Alan said all I needed was to be willing; God would take care of the feelings.

So, I knelt and willingly repeated the words after him. For the next two days, I had inside me the picture of a struggling little girl. It was one thing for my adult mind and will to cooperate with God, and another thing for the little girl to understand and accept what was happening. She seemed to be saying, "I can't! It's not my fault."

Then I had the distinct impression that I was to say the prayer of repentance again. I was in the kitchen; Alan and Beth were out, and Joy was asleep. I stopped what I was doing, went into the bedroom, closed the door and knelt beside the bed. It was very windy outside and the blind was rattling against the window. I began to pray the same prayer I had prayed two days earlier. I noticed the room had grown absolutely quiet and I couldn't hear the wind.

Then, as I prayed, my voice changed from my usual adult voice to the voice of a little girl. It seemed as though I was listening in rather than speaking. At the same time, I saw in my mind a long shaft. I was traveling down it, moving from darkness toward light, like a black and white filmstrip moving very fast. When I reached the end, Jesus was there, sitting with me at His knee. My little-girl voice was still praying.

Jesus asked me to do three things: ask forgiveness for my own occult involvement; forgive my mother; and thank Him for my brother Alan and his influence on my life. As a little girl before Jesus, I had no more need to struggle. My sin was clear to me now and it was right to ask forgiveness. I experienced such peace.

I was jolted back to the present by the loud ringing of the phone. I thought the devil must be interrupting my time with the Lord. The wind was blowing again, I noticed, and the venetian blind was rattling against the window. Still awed by what had just occurred, I went into Alan's study to answer the phone. It was a lady calling with hymns for the Sunday service, and I was prompted to look them up. I read the words of the first hymn.

"It is finished, the battle is over.

It is finished, there'll be no more war.
It is finished, the end of the conflict.
It is finished, and Jesus is Lord!" [1]

Turning to another hymn, I read,

"Tis done, the great transaction's done!
I am the Lord's and He is mine." [2]

Now I was sure God was speaking to me. Eagerly, I turned to the other hymn.

"Down in the human heart,
Crushed by the tempter,
Feelings lie buried that grace can restore;
Touched by a loving hand, wakened by kindness,
Chords that were broken will vibrate once more." [3]

I knew without a doubt what God had done. He had taken me back in time, cleansed me of sin and restored my relationship with Him. The power of Satan in my life was broken.

I expected life to become more normal and all oppression to disappear, but there were still more battles ahead. Weird things began to happen in and around the house. We returned from a holiday to find that our refrigerator was behaving very strangely. Every time I left the kitchen, the refrigerator door opened by itself, but never while I was present. Now, however, we were a little wiser. Even though it seemed crazy to imagine a spirit at work with the refrigerator, we took authority over it in the name of Jesus, commanding it to leave. And it worked!

While we had been on holiday, we had asked the elderly couple next door to come in and feed the cats. The cat food was kept in the refrigerator, but surely there was no connection with Mr. and Mrs. Carlson. They seemed such a nice old couple. Even though they didn't go to church, they had known the previous minister and his wife quite well.

Then one day, Mr. Carlson knocked on our door. He wanted Beth and Joy to stop throwing orange halves onto the middle of his lawn. We assured him they had nothing to do with it. He was back the next day, a little more irritated. He had found more orange halves, uneaten, in exactly the same spot on his lawn. Again we assured him that Beth and Joy were not responsible. The third time, he came back to report that he had found empty milk bottles in exactly the same spot. He was sure that Beth and Joy were playing tricks on him. We were sure they weren't. Again we prayed about it, and the "tricks" stopped.

The oppression on Beth and me continued. There didn't seem to be an end to it, but since being enlightened about satanic oppression, I was able to recondition my thinking. I could say to myself, "It's not me going crazy; it's Satan oppressing me. One day this nightmare will come to an end."

One Saturday while Alan was out gardening, he chatted with Mr. Carlson over the back fence. In the middle of talking about the weather and such things, Mr. Carlson mentioned some experiences he had: automatic writing, visits from spirits during the night, and a list of other occult practices. Alan stood there dazed and horrified.

We could hardly believe it. All this had been going on next door, right under our noses. This sweet little couple was up to their eyebrows in the occult. That explained all the weird occurrences. Satan had a main base of operations for his demons next door.

Now we knew where a lot of the enemy's attack was coming from. Doing something about it was another matter. Alan took some time to pluck up enough courage to confront Mr. Carlson. While they were gardening at the front of the house, Alan told him that all the supernatural things he was doing were of the devil and an abomination to the Lord.

It was Mr. Carlson's turn to be taken aback. And even though he didn't accept Alan's words, Satan's power over our family was broken. The oppression tactics diminished over a period of months until they vanished altogether.

CHAPTER 9

Finally Taking The Plunge

"But you shall receive power
when the Holy Spirit has come upon you."
Acts 1:8

"There must be a better way." These were the words that spontaneously came out of my mouth. We were now entering our second year at West Bexley Church where Alan was gaining a growing experience in pastoral ministry. The church was part of a three-church parish. The Senior Pastor took care of two of the churches and Alan was mainly responsible for the third. Once again he did a bit of everything and he began to try his wings. At seminary, the advice given to students going out to their appointments was: "Take your time the first year to get to know people, understand what's been happening and get settled in. Then you can begin to initiate any new plans."

Alan did that, and by the second year was ready to move forward with a plan for the church. In fact, it was a master plan for the whole year. As an architect would do, he had planned everything in minute detail. After all, you don't start constructing a building without a plan of what the finished building will look like. So Alan had his magnificent plan. He brought me into the study to look at the finished design on a display board on the wall. I stood there looking at it in all its detail. It was then that I couldn't help but utter the words, "There must be a better way."

Despite my discouraging response, Alan pressed on with his plans, but to his dismay his hopes for the church were never fulfilled. It wasn't until a number of years later that he fully understood why. He was at a pastors' conference when Roy Hicks, Sr. from America, recounted a prophetic word that God had given to his denomination in America: "Hitherto you have made your plans and asked Me to bless them, but from now on in I want you to get My plans, for those are the only ones I will bless."

Looking back, Alan realized that, trained as an architect, he was trying to do it an architect's way (i.e., using your creative ideas to come up with your plans). He had to have a renewing of his mind, coming to the place where he asked for God's plans, God's ideas, and God's creative ways of doing things. This marked a major shift in Alan's thinking and approach to ministry. It led him to seek the "revelation" of God as to what the Spirit was saying and what the Spirit wanted him to do. It would completely revolutionize his ministry. Years later he was able to say he never took a major step without receiving a revelation from God and a word from the Lord.

Alan's two years of probationary ministry at West Bexley were over. In October 1969 he was ordained as a Methodist minister. We were looking forward to our next appointment, confident that our trial by fire was behind us and that times could only get better. During these two years at West Bexley, we didn't set the world on fire, but it was a transitional time that prepared us for the next chapter of our life, a chapter that would change our lives forever and position us to fulfill our destiny. It began with a change of location and a ministerial appointment.

Initially, we were offered an appointment out in the country. As we prayed, God directed us not to accept it but to "leave the matter in the hands of the lawful assembly"—to let the Methodist Conference make the decision. God would put us in the right place. To our surprise, the Waverley Methodist Mission, a two-church parish in the Eastern Suburbs of Sydney, put in a request for Alan as assistant pastor. The Conference granted their request, and we were appointed to Waverley where Ronald Coleman was the Senior Pastor.

The Eastern Suburbs, in stark contrast to the quiet suburb of Bexley, was a densely-populated part of the city, crammed between the Pacific Ocean to the east, downtown Sydney to the west, Sydney Harbour to the north, and Botany Bay to the south. We went for a drive to spy out the land and find our future home. The parsonage was an old, dark brick house with a tiny garden and narrow frontage on a busy road.

Everything in the Eastern Suburbs, it seemed, was packed closely together; shops and schools were all within walking distance. We were only minutes from the airport, downtown and half a dozen scenic beaches.

We drove back to Bexley to pack and say our good-byes. It was particularly hard to say good-bye to the ladies in my Bible study group. On the other hand, we weren't sorry to leave Mr. Carlson and the occult practices next door. We were happy that Beth, too, would have a fresh start in a new school.

The Senior Pastor, Ron Coleman, and the people of Lugar Brae Church welcomed us warmly. We moved into Number 12 Leichhardt Street. Its appearance had been quite deceiving. It was long and narrow and actually quite large. Our "gun-barrel house," as Alan described it, was old, dark, shabby and very neglected. We went to work with paint, carpet and curtains. The church trustees provided a builder to help with remodeling. We put the lifeless double mattress in the garage and bought a new one. New carpet replaced the worn-out felt. I made gold pinch-pleated curtains for the living room and hung white crossovers in the bedroom. Number 12 gradually became home.

We spent the first year settling in. Alan's preaching was well received. I became involved in ladies' church aid. When Beth started fourth grade, the new headmaster showed genuine concern for her. He was God's means of restoring her confidence. Joy missed her big sister a great deal when she was at school.

As I grew in my relationship with the Lord, I spent time with Him whenever I could. My heart was stirred to pray for the wider Body of Christ beyond our local Methodist church, and also for the Easter Suburbs. I often knelt beside my bed with my Bible open in front of me and cried out to Him, believing He would speak to me. Jeremiah 33:3 describes it best. *"Call unto me and I will answer you and show you great and mighty things which you do not know."*

I sensed God was about to do something new. He had something on His heart and I wanted to know what it was.

As I sought God in prayer, I felt He showed me that He was going to use Alan in a leadership role to somehow bring the Body of Christ together. How could this be? Alan wasn't even baptized in the Spirit yet, and only thought of being a Methodist minister in the Methodist church. God would have to make it happen.

I was so hungry and thirsty for more teaching and fellowship. I was delighted when, in early 1971, Alan suggested I attend a leaders' seminar. It was organized by

Howard Carter of The Logos Foundation. Alan made the excuse that he was too busy to go, so I went by myself.

Ralph Mahoney and Judson Cornwall from America were speaking. From the first session to the last I drank in every word, like dry, cracked earth receiving rain. I was particularly impressed by Ralph Mahoney's message about Joseph. He talked about Joseph's long wait in prison, about God's preparation of him before he was released as a leader of Egypt. That message stirred the old feeling of destiny. I knew God was preparing Alan and me for some future release.

I went home the first two nights and repeated the messages to Alan. By the third day he decided to hear them for himself. He was as impressed as I was. When the invitation was given to stay for prayer afterward, Alan suggested we remain. We were shown to a small adjacent room to meet Ralph Mahoney and Judson Cornwall. Seated in two elegant chairs, we explained our situation. I told them of God's desire to do a mighty work in the Eastern Suburbs. I began to cry as I shared the burden for unity in the Body of Christ. They explained to me that my crying was a form of intercession. They paced the room for several minutes, speaking in tongues and praying.

I knew without a doubt that Alan and I were called together by God. Now, at last, I thought we could share the same spiritual experience. I could see us holding hands and walking together into a new part of our promised land. I wanted to take Alan's hand, but before I could reach for it, Judson Cornwall spoke to me. "The Lord knows the path you have been on," he said. "He knows the hunger you have for Him. He knows your desire to go forward with Alan, but God's instruction is to wait, submit and rest. God will give you the desire of your heart, but you have to wait." That was hard to hear, but I was reassured—God understood.

Judson Cornwall turned to Alan. God's message to him was the exact opposite. "You are to go forward and take hold of that for which God has taken hold of you. You are to press in and seek God. You must go forward and take the land."

Ralph Mahoney added, "God is planning to use you mightily in the land of Australia."

The picture had changed. I had to let Alan go on alone. At the right time I would join him. But for now, I would wait.

Years later, Ralph Mahoney, in his book, *Is A New Wave of Revival Coming?* recalled the incident this way:

I went to Australia in 1971 for ministry with Judson Cornwall. We had the strong impression that it was God's time to begin fulfilling the prophecy spoken about Australia by Smith Wigglesworth. Back in the early 1930s he prophesied a time would come when God would pour out His Spirit in a mighty way on that country.

Judson and I felt that, as God began moving across the continent, it would result in a gradual increase of spiritual waters, causing rivers to flow in the wilderness.

The situation in Australia in 1971 was very bleak [in Pentecostal churches]. If you could get as many as two hundred people together, you were having a phenomenal success.

If a man had pastored for thirty years and worked hard at it, he might have thirty members; or if forty years, he might have forty members. With a few notable exceptions, it was a country that just was not yielding fruit. Men labored and prayed and sought the Lord, and yet results were meager and ministry very, very difficult.

In that first 1971 leaders' conference in the city of Sydney, a number of the key men the Lord intended to use in the decade that was ahead were present.

> *At the end of the first meeting, Judson Cornwall and I were asked to go in and pray for a particular brother. As we laid hands upon him, the Spirit of the Lord came and we began to prophesy over this man the great things that God was going to do through him in the nation of Australia.* [1]

I was greatly encouraged by the words from Judson Cornwall and Ralph Mahoney, not only for me but also for Alan. It was reassuring to know God was at work. All I needed to do now was to wait, submit, and rest.

Alan had first heard of the Pentecostal Movement in 1956 when healing evangelist Oral Roberts came to Australia. In 1963, during his days as a student pastor in Greenacre, he read about the strange phenomenon of tongues in a popular magazine. Then there was Mrs. Knight, who attended his Methodist church in the morning and went a quarter-mile down the road to a garage in the evening. That garage was home for a little Pentecostal church led by an Australian pastor who had studied at Life Bible College in Los Angeles, married an American and returned to start a church. Alan met Pastor Don Baker only once in his five years at Greenacre. They chose the same moment to visit Mrs Knight at home. It was hard to tell who was more uncomfortable. Little did Alan realize that Don Baker would later become a close friend and a member of his board of directors.

It was beyond Alan's understanding why anyone would choose to attend a tiny service in a garage lit by a kerosene lamp. The Methodist church, after all, had a nice building, electricity and a larger congregation. Mrs. Knight was only too ready to explain. She loaned Alan books and tapes by Pastor Norm Armstrong. She told him about the Holy Spirit. Alan read the books and listened to the stories and the tapes. He considered himself an evangelical, conservative, Bible-believing Christian, but one with an open mind—or so he thought. So he went to the Bible and restudied the gifts and the baptism in the Holy Spirit.

He came to the conservative, dispensational, evangelical conclusion that these experiences were _not_ for today. They were only to get the church going—to launch the ship, so to speak. His response at the time was more or less: "I don't need anything more. I'm happy the way I am. I've got a lovely wife, a beautiful daughter, a home I designed myself. I'm studying in seminary and working in a church. My life is full—what else do I need?"

He threw buckets of cold water over that dear woman! She eventually left the Methodist church and joined the Pentecostal church down the road. Alan was relieved. He wanted nothing to do with that "crazy sect." He could imagine the weird things that went on there: swinging from the chandeliers and rolling on the floor. He intended to keep his distance so he wouldn't be zapped by some strange experience he didn't want. Years later Alan had a happy reunion with Mrs. Knight.

The Lord had not given up, however. He was going to get Alan's attention one way or another. Alan is fond of telling a story about a mule:

> *There once was a man who owned a stubborn mule. That mule wouldn't do anything the man wanted. If he wanted it to stand up, it would sit down. If he wanted it to sit down, it would stand up.*

So he took it to a man who trained mules. "Can you train my mule?"

"Sure," the mule trainer said.

He put the mule in a corral and explained that he would start with step one. The owner asked, "What's step one?"

"Just wait and see."

The trainer picked up a two-by-four and walked over to the mule. The mule kept right on staring into space. The trainer clobbered him over the head with the piece of timber.

The owner was most upset. "What are you doing to my mule?"

"That's step one in mule-training. First, you get their attention!"

When God wants your attention, He tickles you with a feather. If you take no notice, He hits you over the head with a two-by-four, even though the hands that hold the two by four are hands of love. God used Mrs. Knight as the feather treatment, and Alan took no notice.

Four years later, it was time for the two-by-four treatment. In 1967, Alan's life fell apart. Around the time of Joy's birth, he cried out to God, "There must be something more!" He didn't find that "something more" for another four years, but the journey had begun.

In 1968, while at West Bexley, the young man who had given us a book by John Sherrill, *They Speak With Other Tongues,* began to tell Alan stories and lend him other books. He urged him to read *The Cross and the Switchblade* about David Wilkerson's ministry in Teen Challenge in New York. Alan finished it, admitting, "Dear God, that man has something

I don't have. He's got a power in his life and ministry that I don't possess. I don't see it in the lives around me. Lord, that's the 'something else' I need."

It was one thing for Alan to know what he needed and quite another to be willing to receive it. The fact that he was a minister, a graduate of theological seminary, only increased his resistance. A minister is supposed to know his Bible. His biggest problem, he realized finally, wasn't tongues or baptism or Pentecost, it was pride.

His willingness, to start with, had some conditions attached. "Lord, I'll receive this experience—but on my terms. Privately, Lord, just between You and me, so it won't rock the church boat. And also I don't want the tongues bit, Lord." This bargaining process was to last three years.

In January 1971, during a vacation at our beach house, he reached the end of himself, crying out desperately, "Lord, I can't go on any further. Either I make a breakthrough this year, or I may as well give up the ministry and go back to architecture. I just can't see enough evidence of Your power in my life."

Within two months he was baptized in the Holy Spirit. Soon after the ministry from Judson Cornwall and Ralph Mahoney in March 1971, a pastor friend, Don Evans, called Alan to tell him about his own experience with the Baptism in the Holy Spirit. There was a Catholic Charismatic prayer meeting on the Sydney University campus; would Alan be interested in coming? We went, despite Alan's prejudice regarding Catholics. At that point, Alan considered that Catholic beliefs were not in line with orthodox, evangelical theology; he was not sure that a Catholic could even be saved. He never forgot the first time he sat down with his senior pastor, Ron Coleman, who told him, "Now that you're in the

Eastern Suburbs of Sydney" [an area that was predominantly Roman Catholic and Jewish] "you will have to learn to work with Catholics." Alan's unspoken reaction was "Never!"

The Waverly Methodist Mission had a strong working relationship with the local Catholic church. Indeed, it was so unique that when Ron Coleman visited the Vatican in 1972, he had a one-on-one meeting with the Pope. In early 1971, Alan was still somewhat gun shy of involvement with Catholics. It was an indication of Alan's desperation that he accepted the invitation to go to a Catholic Charismatic prayer meeting.

So, Alan found himself sitting in St. Michael's chapel. He had the sensation of hesitating on the edge of deep water, wondering whether to jump or not. When the invitation to receive the Baptism was given, he "jumped." After the service we went back into the church kitchen with a few others and there Dr. Alex Reichel, Associate Professor of Applied Mathematics at the University of Sydney, explained the basics of the Baptism in the Holy Spirit. Then he laid hands on Alan and prayed. Almost immediately, Alan began to speak in tongues, unemotionally and rather loudly. We laughed about it later—a Methodist evangelical receiving a Pentecostal experience in a Catholic prayer meeting. Church unity!

Then it was my turn for prayer. I was expecting a release to speak in tongues, but that was to come later. Instead, to my surprise, I began to laugh, a well of joy overflowing from deep inside me. I laughed and laughed. I was drunk in the Spirit, and it wasn't until we got outside that I was able to stand up straight by myself.

The waiting was over. Now Alan and I could move forward together. We had taken the first step. The second step came a month later at a small home meeting, when we heard Jim Glennon, Canon of St. Andrews Cathedral in downtown

Sydney, talk of the need for leadership in the renewal. In his clipped British accent, he announced, "Somebody will have to nail their colors to the mast, come out into the open and take a stand."

Alan took the challenge. As we walked from the house where this meeting had been held, across the tree-lined street to the car, he exclaimed, "Dear God, let me be that man!"

So far he had only shared his experience with one or two others. At the next church service at Lugar Brae, he stood in front of the congregation and preached openly about the Baptism in the Holy Spirit, telling them about his experience.

His sermon sent shock waves through the congregation. A few were glad that their pastor was speaking out boldly about this new experience. The rest were completely taken aback by what seemed to them to be an experience totally foreign to their Methodist background.

Alan remembered a speaker one time saying that, "after you have received the Baptism of the Holy Spirit, you ought to be locked up for a year because you are dangerous." It simply pointed out that when one has a dynamic encounter with God, we tend to think and expect everyone else to want and receive the same thing. Sad to say, we tend to be a bit fanatical and dogmatic—so strongly is our belief reinforced by our own personal experience. Later, Alan realized this was a lesson to learn. He has since shared with others how at the time, he was filled with zeal but not with wisdom. He did not do things in a loving way. Consequently, he hurt people unintentionally. He was so caught up in the enthusiasm of his new Pentecostal experience, he kept pushing onward in spite of criticism.

Years later he was invited back to speak in the Lugar Brae Church once more. The following excerpt from an article Alan wrote for Vision magazine describes what happened that Sunday.

During the time I was a minister in the early 1970s, when the charismatic renewal broke in Australia, I hurt people because I lacked the wisdom to know how to handle the new dimension of the Spirit that had touched mine and other lives. In my naïve enthusiasm I tried to push people into that same experience instead of lovingly leading them. The inevitable happened. People got hurt, and mostly it was my fault, although I didn't realize it at the time.

So on this Sunday I was back in the pulpit again and I felt I should speak on the subject of the two signs Jesus gave that would cause the world to take notice—love and unity. Half way through the service, just as I was at the Communion table, it seemed as though the Lord said to me, "You can't just talk about love, you have to demonstrate it. Ask the people to forgive you for what you did five years ago, when you hurt so many of them."

So I did just that at the end of the sermon, and then it happened! When I finished speaking the senior layman of the church stood up and asked me to forgive them also. We had communion together, then everyone came to the front of the church to sing the last hymn. I tell you, there weren't too many dry eyes in the place.

When the service was finished I went to each of the people who had been there five years before and simply said, "Would you forgive me for what I did?" One lady (the organist) summed it up concerning what I had done years before when she said, "Alan, you made us feel that if we didn't accept this new charismatic renewal, we weren't really Christians."

I couldn't help but think of Michael Harper's words: "Division caused in the churches through the charismatic renewal would never have happened if our love had been genuine."

That Sunday, not only tears, but genuine love and forgiveness flowed as God healed the hurts and scars of past encounters.

The year 1971 proved to be a breakthrough year. Now that Alan was baptized in the Holy Spirit, there was an accelerated thrust forward. We were about to enter an entirely new dimension of our faith walk. There was soon to be a very necessary step that would lead to the discovery of God's assignment for us.

CHAPTER 10

The Carrot
In Front of The Donkey

*"Many are the plans in the mind of a man,
but it is the purpose of the Lord that will be
established."*
Proverbs 19:21 (RSV)

The Langstaff family had its home in a rather colorful and diverse part of Sydney. In it lived the very wealthy as well as those of more modest means. It included the famous Bondi Beach and the infamous red light district of Kings Cross, both just minutes from our home. Parts of the Eastern Suburbs had a reputation for drug trafficking, prostitution, and organized crime.

In 1968, Alan had read *The Cross and The Switchblade,* David Wilkerson's story of his outreach in the streets of New York. The book had challenged him a great deal and it was natural that he should see possibilities of a similar outreach in the Eastern Suburbs. If it could happen in New York, it could happen here. Now, three years later and newly baptized in the Spirit, Alan gathered a group of leaders to pray and discuss the idea of a Teen Challenge-type ministry in Sydney.

Looking at such a diverse group, one would not naturally link them to drug addicts. It included Canon Jim Glennon, an Anglican with an outstanding healing ministry, whose tall figure and clerical dress brought a touch of traditional respectability. There was dear Father Gerald Hawkins, the elderly leader of the Catholic prayer meeting at St. Michael's. Alex Reichel, Catholic lay leader and professor, accompanied him. Dean Sherman, Australian director of YWAM, and Noel Bell, an architect, were also present, the latter known for his huge bear hugs. Other members were Janet Hemans from St Andrew's, Doug McFaddyen of Full Gospel Businessmen's Fellowship, and local pastors Alan Alcock and David Crawford. There was also a gentleman named Alan Wales, who was to play an important part later in this story. The only person in the group who was directly involved with rehabilitation was Enid Crowther from Moombara, a residential community that ministered to troubled people. Last, but not least, a group of seven dedicated young people gave a healthy balance to all the weight of years and experience.

Some of these men and women had been in the Charismatic Renewal for years, unlike Alan, who was a complete newcomer. They were therefore cautious to begin with. But the need for a Teen Challenge-type ministry in Sydney was glaringly obvious, so they gave him all the encouragement and support they could. After several meetings, they agreed Alan should visit New York and see Teen Challenge firsthand, and if possible, I should join him in the States.

I sat in the last meeting and knew that God was working in everything. But in my heart, I had a deep conviction that Alan was not called to a Teen Challenge ministry. In retrospect, we would be able to see that God was using the idea like a carrot in front of a donkey; God got Alan going just enough to stumble onto His real plan for his life.

The passage of scripture shared by one of the young people also suggested that God had something else in mind. It was the story of Nehemiah and how he organized the rebuilding of the walls of Jerusalem. She felt it applied to Alan and to the building and repairing ministry that God would give him in the Body of Christ.

The group laid hands on Alan and me and prayed. Under the anointing of the Spirit, 17-year-old Ray Nelson Hauer began to prophesy. "Even as you have called My people together, you will blow the trumpet and call My people together again, for you will rebuild the walls."

At this significant moment, we knew that God had put a divine stamp of approval on the trip. It didn't matter that we were so young in the things of the Spirit and so limited in our understanding.

In the same moment, the Lord told Ray that he was also to go to America, but not with Alan. He shared the idea later, and after praying together, Alan agreed. Ray was not a typical 17-year-old. He was spiritually gifted far beyond his years. He was living by faith together with a community of young people called Lifegate, who met daily to pray, share, fellowship and seek the Lord.

Enthusiastically, Alan began to plan his itinerary. At first it was centered around Teen Challenge, until Alan had a conversation with Ray Muller, an Anglican minister from New Zealand, who just happened to be passing through Sydney on his way to England. Three different people told Alan he should talk to Ray. By the third time, Alan knew God was trying to get his attention. So he went to hear Ray Muller at St. Michael's, and spoke to him on the phone the next day. That strategic phone call not only set the itinerary in order, it set the direction of the ministry for many years to come.

"I'm going to England to work with Michael Harper," Ray said with his New Zealand accent. "Michael is an Anglican minister who has been called by God to leave his parish work and begin a ministry called The Fountain Trust. He believes God wants to bring unity and renewal to all the denominations of the Body of Christ." As Alan listened intently, he felt a stirring within him. "The Fountain Trust is holding an international Charismatic conference in Guilford, England," Ray continued, "and it would be great if you could be there."

Alan's mind was beginning to race. He realized that God was speaking to him through Ray Muller. Ray had another suggestion: "Why don't you visit the Church of the Redeemer in Houston, Texas, while you are in America? The community is led by Graham Pulkingham, and it's experiencing tremendous renewal."

Ray went on to share that his own ministry, Christian Advance Ministries, was planning a national Charismatic conference in New Zealand in January 1973. When Alan heard that, the Holy Spirit conceived something in his mind. He found himself saying excitedly, "We should have a similar conference in Sydney—a national Charismatic conference."

The trip to America was taking on new meaning. It became apparent that Alan would spend less time studying drug rehabilitation and more time being exposed to the Charismatic Renewal worldwide. God was bringing His plan into focus.

So our first big faith venture began. It was truly a faith venture as Alan needed $2,000 for his round-the-world fare and we had no money to pay for it. He had been given a tape to listen to by a friend. It was a message by Harald Bredesen given at a church Alan had never heard of called Melodyland Christian Center in Anaheim, California. In the midst of the message Harald quoted Philippians 4:19; *"And my God shall supply all your need according to His riches in glory by Christ Jesus."*

It was as if those words were written in six-foot high letters on a wall. For Alan, it was a personal promise regarding the trip.

He had a number of needs, the first being money. The church kindly offered to pay Alan's wages in his absence while I took care of meetings and services—but Alan's wages would not cover an around-the-world trip. We knew it was entirely up to God. We told people about Alan's planned trip but said nothing of the financial need.

The first encouraging sign came from the government—a $100 tax rebate. Then, about this time, we had a visit from an American couple who were millionaires. We thought, *At last, Lord, here is your opportunity to solve all our problems!* I even had a dream in which I saw a check made out to us for quite a large sum of money. I felt as though I was walking around with dollar signs in my eyes, even though I didn't say a thing. The millionaire couple came, spent a pleasant afternoon, and went. That was all. We learned that God wanted us to put our trust in Him, not in man.

Alan's mother, Scottish by birth and also by nature, couldn't understand how God could provide the money as we believed for it to come. One day she was visiting our home and we were discussing this when the postman blew his whistle as he put letters in our mailbox. When Alan returned with the mail, he opened up a letter in front of his mother that held a check for $500 from the Catholic prayer group meeting at St. Michael's. This helped not only Alan, but also his mother to believe God would do it. Money kept coming in a variety of wonderful ways.

The other major need Alan had was for a traveling companion. He had never flown anywhere in his life before and, consequently, had never been outside of Australia. In fact, he had been out of the state of New South Wales only twice, once to a convention and once on our honeymoon. You could almost say he had never been anywhere. God provided a wonderful traveling companion, a pharmacist by the name of David Reekes, who was involved with the Moombara Community that ministered to troubled people. David wanted to visit similar places and the ministries that Alan wanted to see, so it was a perfect match.

The itinerary was finally completed. Alan would fly first to England via Israel and Rome, and then to America—a reversal of his original plan to go straight to Teen Challenge in New York. When the day came for the final arrangements to be completed with the travel agent, Alan was up early. He sat down at his desk and worked out what he needed for his fare and traveler's checks. Then he added up all the money he had received. He was $25 short.

Later that morning, a shrill blast of a whistle announced the arrival of the postman. Alan wasted no time getting out to the mailbox. One of the letters held a check—and the check was for, what else, but $25. The amount was complete. Alan was able to keep his appointment and pay his fare.

When he arrived home, I was at the back of the house preparing the evening meal. He walked into the kitchen with a big smile on his face.

"It's all fixed up! I have my tickets, praise the Lord!" His voice had the same ring of victory as if he was announcing that his favorite team, Canterbury Bankstown, had won a football game. He rubbed his hands together as if to say, "That's a good job done!" He went on, "You know, Harry's been really great, making all these arrangements for me when he didn't know if I would get the money."

I agreed. After all, Harry Hollister, our travel agent, was accustomed to the more conventional traveler, and I don't think he knew what he was letting himself in for when he got tangled up with the Langstaffs.

Alan turned to go and then stopped and said very deliberately, "I felt I should book seats for you and the girls to fly out on Friday, August 13, at 7 p.m., six weeks from now. Harry thought it was a good idea, too."

"You really think I should go?" I asked, surprised.

"Yes," he replied. "I believe the Lord wants you, Beth and Joy to meet me in America."

It seemed to me that God was giving me a choice. Either I could comply with Alan's conviction, or I could politely say, "Well, I'd rather not, thank you." I felt no pressure from God to go or to stay; I was reassured that God would lead me to make the right decision.

Go to America? I mused, turning the whole idea over in my mind. It was a brand-new thought to me. *Maybe I would go and take the girls. But what about the money? I don't need to decide right away—or do I? Alan is leaving next week. What do you want me to do, Lord? Stay or go? Show me, God...*

I think it's GO!

CHAPTER 11

Crucible of Faith

"And my God shall supply all your need
according to His riches in glory by Christ Jesus."
Philippians 4:19

In the Sunday service before Alan left, I was overcome with tears and had to go home. Perhaps I sensed some of the trauma that lay ahead.

Alan's departure date came. He had received more money over the last weekend, some of which he spent buying film for his camera. Then he gave me his last ten dollars for our tickets to America. There was great excitement as the whole family took Alan to the airport that Tuesday. Even his Mum was there.

I shall never forget Alan's parting words. "See you in America!"

The harsh reality of my situation didn't penetrate right then. The moment of truth came the next morning. The girls had gone to school and all was quiet in the parsonage until the phone rang. I recognized Harry's cheerful voice on the line.

"Well, did Alan get off all right?" he inquired.

"Yes, everything went fine."

"Look," he said, "Why don't you come into town and see me? As an act of faith, we can start making arrangements for your trip." Harry and Alan had booked a package deal of 13 days for Beth, Joy and me. Ray Nelson Hauer would travel with us and we would all meet Alan in Los Angeles. I would need approximately $1,500 for airfares and accommodations, not including meals. I had no money except the ten dollars Alan had given me, but Harry's confident air made me agree without question.

I really appreciated Harry's encouragement. After all, it had been relatively easy agreeing and praying with Alan for his fare, but this was a different matter. Alan had gone and now it was my turn. I needed a boost to get me going. There was a lot to be done and I listened carefully to Harry's instructions.

"You'll have to get smallpox vaccinations. And we'll need to go to work immediately on your passport application, there's so little time before you're due to leave."

I didn't know it, but God was about to give me my first big faith lesson in His ability to provide for my needs. It was one thing to know the promise, *"My God shall supply all your needs,"* and believe it in my mind. It was another thing altogether to be placed in a crucible of experience where that promise would be written indelibly on my heart. I had to learn, in a new way, that God is a God who provides. I knew that already, but I had never been forced to trust God alone for my financial needs. Now my faith had an opportunity to grow, because I had a need that only God could supply. I would soon discover how God works to manifest His strength in my weakness.

It was exciting when God began to send a steady flow of money. People were led to give, sometimes a few dollars, sometimes more. The beautiful thing about it was that each gift told its own story of God and the giver. One of the first gifts came from our young friend Ray. He had received $276 toward his airfare, but he decided to give the money to me, keeping just enough to cover his passport expenses. I objected until I realized the Lord was leading him, and then I accepted it.

Two days later, Ray was having dinner with us. A young man came to the door, looking for him. There, right before my eyes, I saw the verse, *"Give, and it will be given to you," (Luke 6:38)* demonstrated. The young man had emptied his bank account to give all his savings to Ray. To the last dollar, it was the exact amount that Ray needed: $769—$766 for his airfare and $3 for the airport tax. Ray's gift to me was returned to him multiplied, and God had arranged for it to take place in front of me to encourage my faith.

Another encouragement was the way the Lord took care of our smallpox vaccinations; we had only a small bump on our arms, and no pain or fever. This was a miracle for Beth, a ten-year-old asthmatic with a history of severe allergies and reactions. Little Joy, who was four, would run into the kitchen, hold up her arm and say, "Prayer, Mummy." And then add, "It's better now," and go off happily to kindergarten or play. The doctor was surprised when we reported back with no ill effects.

By now, our departure date, Friday, August 13, was two and a half weeks away. We had been given a lot of money, but we needed much more. I prayed about that one morning as I sat in the kitchen and sipped tea from my favorite china cup. I had a custom of making morning tea a time of fellowship with the Lord. I prayed a quiet, matter-of-fact prayer. "Lord, I believe you want the children and I to go to America, but I need a lot more money. It would be nice and it would strengthen my faith if you could arrange for some money to come every day—even a little bit—right up until the day I have to pay for my tickets. You don't have to, Lord, but it'd be nice if you did."

Whether He answered that prayer or not, I knew there was enough evidence that He wanted me to go. I wasn't twisting God's arm saying, "Do this or else!" I was simply asking for encouragement.

Each day from then on, an amount of money came, sometimes in the mail, sometimes from people I met. On one occasion, our dear friend, Noel Bell, was visiting. We had a rich evening of fellowship and prayer, and it was nearly midnight when he got up to leave. The thought occurred to me that God was cutting things close; there had been nothing in the letterbox and nothing given to me all day. And here it was, two minutes to 12. Noel and I walked up the narrow hall to the front door, trying to be quiet so we wouldn't disturb the children. He paused at the door, and reached out his hand to shake mine. I thought he was being rather formal, but took his hand anyway. As I did, I felt something in my palm and heard the crinkling sound of paper.

"A little something for you," Noel said.

I looked down and found I was holding a check for $200. I thanked him and with that he was gone. He left me not only grateful for his generosity, but also grateful to God for His faithfulness. I had such a warm, cared-for feeling, as if God was saying, "I love you! Trust Me! Even if the hour grows late and it seems like I have forgotten, I will still come." I felt so reassured of His love that I was glad He had kept me waiting all day so He could show me He loved me in a personal way.

On Sunday, nothing came. No one had given me anything at church and there was no mail delivery. I didn't go around saying "I need money," but in my mind, I was looking for it everywhere. It had to turn up somehow! I stayed up late, but still nothing. I finally prepared for bed. I had to go back to the kitchen for something and felt a little lonely. Putting out the lights, I made my way back to the bedroom. With every step my trust waned and my doubts became stronger. Then, as I passed the front door, something caught my eye. Something was sticking out from under it. I bent down and picked up a ten-dollar bill. I never found out who put it there, but, praise God, He had done it again! *Every day He is faithful. When will I ever learn to trust Him?*

It was Friday, August 6, one week before our departure date, and I didn't have nearly enough money. I had witnessed the Lord supply Alan's fare one week in advance, but it wasn't happening for me. So I came to the conclusion that I couldn't go. Rather reluctantly, I called Harry, the travel agent.

His cheerful voice came on the line. "How are things going? Do you have all the money, yet?"

"No," I replied hesitantly. I half expected him to tell me it was all off.

"That's all right," Harry said. "Come in on Monday and we will fix it up then."

It was such a blessing to have a Christian travel agent. God was not only working in our lives, but also in Harry's. Over the weeks, we had many opportunities to talk about Jesus and the reality of the Holy Spirit in our lives. A light of hope and expectation replaced the longing look in his eyes. As a result of seeing the reality of God in our experiences, he fully committed himself to Jesus. He had been a Methodist minister before he became a travel agent, and he reentered the ministry, a different person.

Harry had a heart condition at the time of our trip and he continued to suffer with it. But he wasn't worried. As he said to me after an operation, "You know, although my heart condition has not been healed, the Lord's operation on my spiritual heart condition has been successful."

That was the important thing. When he died of a heart attack some years later, we could look back and thank God for the deep and permanent work that he had done in Harry's life. We could not see at the time the full extent of what God was doing in all the events surrounding this trip of destiny.

So my positive confession of faith continued. And so did my apprehension. I was far from resting in faith, but I clung to the verse that the Lord had given us, *"My God shall supply all your need."* Thank God that when questions about the money came, He anointed me so I could laugh at the situation, and He set a seal on my lips so that I couldn't utter one word of doubt to anyone.

It was Monday of the last week. The mailman made his delivery, but there was no miracle check this time. Rather embarrassed, I called Harry.

"I still don't have enough money."

Unexpectedly, he said, "That's okay. Give me a call tomorrow."

I am sure that Harry thought he was doing me a good turn. In actual fact, he was only prolonging the agony.

On Tuesday, the same thing happened. Certainly God was being faithful, and each day an amount of money would come. But I was getting more and more anxious. Also, I felt terribly alone. I couldn't share my anxiety with anyone.

I had felt impressed from the beginning that I wasn't to go about telling people of my need. The Lord gave me grace to confess positively that I was going to America, even when I was full of doubts inside. Outwardly, it appeared that all was well, and it did not occur to many people to ask if I had all the money for the fare. They took it for granted that sensible people only planned an overseas trip if they could afford it.

I had to continually act and talk as if everything was all right. I had no one to talk to, which was probably just as well; it stopped me from saying anything negative. I was facing the giant of my own fear—fear that God would fail me at the last moment, when I needed Him most. The struggle between this fear and faith made me feel as though I had aged ten years. My children, Beth and Joy, were too young to share my struggle, though they had emptied their money boxes of the little they had, which in God's eyes was a big thing to do.

By Wednesday, I was praying, "Lord, please make Harry tell me it's all off. I can't stand it any longer!" But Harry didn't.

By Thursday, I fully expected Harry to say, "Look, this is going too far." But no! Harry, uninvolved in the emotional trauma, had more faith than I did at that point. He told me again, "Come in tomorrow." "Tomorrow" was Friday, August 13, the day I was supposed to be leaving!

Friday. D-day! This was it. By the end of the day I would know if the whole wild plan was going to work or not.

Nothing arrived in the mail. No one came. I was only $150 short, but without that $150 I had no tickets and no trip. I was due at the travel agent's at 3 p.m. with the money. Ray had offered to drive me there. He already had his tickets, of course. If only I could have received the money in one lump sum like he had, I thought, it would have made things so much easier.

The hours raced by. The children were at school and I was alone. By 12 noon, I was in a turmoil of fear and panic. I had to do something! Perhaps I could call Alan's superintendent and ask for an advance on his wages. Perhaps the bank would give me a loan; we knew the manager reasonably well. I gave in to temptation and dialed the number of the bank. My heart was pounding hard enough to burst. The line was busy. I tried again—still no success.

"All right, Lord," I said, "if it's still busy the third time, I'll give up trying to get a loan."

It was still busy. I knew I had no alternative but to wait for God, regardless of my fear. He would surely deliver on time. That should have given me peace, but it didn't. I felt like I was going to explode with all the pressure. I didn't dare leave the house, even though I was supposed to pick up some notices at the church office. The money might arrive while I was out! I decided I had better pack. I went around the house, threw clothes into suitcases, leaving them open on the bed. I dressed, ready for the trip, and put my coat out. At the last minute I stuffed the children's teddy bears into a string bag.

It was 2 p.m. I had put off leaving the house as long as possible, but now I would just have to risk it. I had to visit a woman in the hospital to take her some flowers and tell her that I was going to America for the next two weeks. I managed to convince her that everything was fine, though I couldn't convince myself.

From the hospital, I drove to the church office in Bondi Junction. I had never prayed so urgently in all my life as I did then, praying in English as well as practicing the few words I was able to speak in tongues. I hurried into the church office and found it deserted. I was in a dilemma. I had to get the notices, but I also had to get home at once in case someone came with money, and in time to get to the travel agent's by 3 p.m. Agitated, I waited. No one appeared. In contrast to my desperate hurry, everything else seemed to be moving in slow motion.

Then a tall figure appeared in the doorway. I recognized a good friend, Alan Wales. Two weeks earlier, he had stood on my doorstep, prayed for me and rebuked Satan soundly for hanging on to my fare money. I had no idea what he was doing in the church office, but I knew I must not show what a turmoil I was in. *God, help me!*

All of a sudden, I saw my notices sitting on the secretary's desk. Now I could hurry back home. But to my dismay, Alan Wales began to chat.

"How are the arrangements for the trip going?"

I said the opposite of what I felt. "Oh, good."

"The time's coming close isn't it?"

"Yes," I said, "it's today."

"Well," Alan said, "I didn't realize." Then he asked, "You've been believing God for the fare, haven't you?"

My "yes" was rather strained.

He persisted with the questioning. "Have you got all the money yet?"

"Well, no," I admitted. "Not quite."

"How much do you still need?"

"$150, I think," I told him reluctantly.

"That's really strange," he said. "Two days ago, I was praying for you and I had a distinct impression that I should give you $150. I thought it was the devil's idea, but now I know it was from God." I could hardly believe my ears. "I'll go straight out to my van and write you a check."

I followed him outside and watched him write a check for $160. I asked what the extra $10 was for.

He gave a knowing smile. "I think you'll need it."

I can't describe the feeling of release. I actually had the money! Thoughts raced through my mind as I hurriedly drove home. I was amazed to see how God chose to answer my prayer. My need was met while I was carrying out a seemingly unimportant duty, picking up notices for the Sunday church service.

I couldn't stop praising God. He had planned it all. He knew that I would be at the church office at precisely the same time as Alan Wales. He had arranged for the secretary to be gone so that we would have a chance to talk. He had even told Alan the amount that I needed. And to think I hadn't wanted to leave the house to pick up those notices!

My money worries were over. All I needed to do now was to gather my thoughts together and get going, fast. I was still in a daze, so that was not going to be easy.

Ray and Nanna, Alan's mother, were waiting for me at home. Ray was worried because we should have been in town by that time. Nanna still didn't fully understand what was going on, but she was ready to help in anyway she could. I asked her to pick up Beth and Joy at school and bring them home to get ready. I felt I should change my shoes and take my good handbag with me, thinking it would save time later.

Ray and I left for the travel agent's. We made a hasty stop at the bank to withdraw the money from my savings account. I stuffed it into my bag together with the money I had collected at home. By now, the afternoon traffic was getting heavy, particularly so because it was Friday. Our journey into the heart of downtown Sydney was not the quickest or the easiest, but we made it safely. We entered the travel agency triumphantly. Harry was waiting at his desk.

His first excited question was, "You've got the money?"

I tipped it all out in front of him. "I think so! I've brought it all, so I hope there is enough."

He began counting at once. "We'd better hurry! I haven't made out the tickets yet."

I prayed quietly that there would be enough. Harry announced matter of factly, "You are $23 short."

Oh Lord, I thought. *What do I do now?* Surely after coming this far, I had to have all the money. Then the thought came, *Look inside your purse.* I obeyed and pulled out a small bundle of notes, housekeeping money left over from shopping. I counted it.

I was smiling when I looked up. "Here you are, Harry. I have exactly $23 in my purse." I sat back in my chair, hardly able to believe that this was happening. I had never experienced anything like it before.

Ray had been sitting there quietly, but now he seemed a little uneasy. I saw him glance soberly at his watch, then at Harry behind the desk and finally at me. "I'll have to go soon," he said. "Someone's picking me up at my flat at five to take me to the airport."

I thought, *He can't go! How would I ever get home to pick up the children and the luggage?* A horrible, lonely, hopeless feeling invaded my heart.

Harry was feverishly trying to get the tickets together. Now it was his turn to get in a dither. "If only I'd made out the tickets earlier," he said. "I should have known you were coming, but we're not supposed to write out tickets until they are paid for."

I felt sorry for Harry, caught in the middle of this with all the responsibility on him. I was concerned about his heart condition, too. I knew he was on tranquilizers, and this situation wasn't exactly conducive to tranquility! Harry was used to pressure in his work, but never anything like this.

The pressure was showing. "You'd better pray for these tickets," he said, "that I don't make some terrible mistake. I can't think straight!"

I quietly prayed and claimed God's covering on the tickets. He called a colleague to check them, and sure enough, she discovered some serious mistakes. Praise God, He answered prayer - otherwise those tickets would never have taken us to our destination.

Ray was looking at his watch again. "I'm sorry to leave you here with no transport, but I must go now." The peak-hour traffic was getting heavier by the minute and if he didn't go, he wouldn't make it in time.

"That's all right, I understand," I replied, trying to appear calm. "I'll see you at the airport."

I was alone again, dependent on the Lord. Surely He wouldn't fail me now, so close to the goal. All the prayer and believing and agony of the last few days couldn't be for nothing. But God, it seemed, was requiring one more supreme effort of trust and faith.

At 4:45 p.m., I sat there trying to calculate how long it would take to get home and to the airport by 6 p.m. In peak-hour traffic on a Friday afternoon, I didn't know how I was going to do it. If only there was more time.

Harry guessed my thoughts. "You're supposed to go home and get the girls, aren't you?"

"Yes," I answered.

"Well, I'll call and order you a taxi."

Even if I got a taxi, it would be cutting it very fine, but what else could I do? I had to go home and get the girls—or did I? I had a moment of truth; I would have to go straight to the airport. I knew now why I had felt impressed to change my shoes and get ready before I left home. I had to act decisively as every moment counted.

"Can I use the phone, Harry? I have to call home." I dialed the number, praying, *God, help them to understand. Please don't let them panic.*

Someone picked up the phone, and I heard Nanna's Scottish accent.

"Hello?" she said.

"Hello, Nanna."

"Is that you, Dorothy?" she asked, surprised to hear my voice.

"Nanna, I'm running late and won't be able to get home. I'm going straight to the airport, and I want you all to meet me there."

Fortunately, Pam, a responsible woman from church, had offered to take us to the airport and she was there by then. I explained briefly to Beth, asked her to take care of Joy, and then spoke to Pam.

Her familiar voice was calm. "What do you want me to do?" she asked. I told her to close the suitcases and fetch my cream-colored coat. She did everything I said and returned to the phone. "What now?"

"Now take Nanna, Beth and Joy and the luggage—don't forget the string bag of teddy bears—and put them all in the car, and I will see you at the airport."

"Right!" she said, "We'll leave as soon as we can."

Praise God, Pam didn't criticize me in any way, even though she may not have understood or approved of everything

I was doing. She knew God was with me and in a mature and efficient way offered her support.

Harry, meanwhile, had completed the tickets correctly, found me a Qantas carry bag and was still trying for a taxi. It was twenty past five.

"There was at least a 20-minute wait for taxis," he said, "probably longer, since it's peak hour. So that idea's no good."

I was sitting there looking helpless, and Harry knew it was his turn to act. "Come on." He thrust the Qantas bag into my hand, took my other arm firmly and steered me through the office and out into the busy street. "I'm going to get you a taxi."

There was no taxi in sight. Not one. Only bumper-to-bumper cars, waiting for their turn at the intersection.

"Where are we going?" I asked, as he propelled me across the street.

"I think I know where I can get you a taxi!"

By this time, we were both running along the sidewalk. We raced into the back of the Wentworth Hotel, speeding noiselessly over the thick red carpet. We reached the front foyer, and right before our eyes was the answer to our prayer—a taxi! We stopped short. Then Harry hurried over to the doorman and explained my desperate predicament.

The doorman stood stiffly in his fine uniform and said in a posh voice, "I'm sorry, sir, but it's only for the clientele."

The terrible look of disappointment that crossed our faces must have moved him to make an exception to the rule.

"Just a moment," he said. He crossed over to the taxi and bent down to speak to the driver. We couldn't hear their conversation, but we prayed that God would make a way where there was no way. It seemed like ages before he came back.

"Well, the driver normally takes the opposite route to the North Shore. But he's agreed to take you to the airport."

"Oh, thank you!" I was smiling from ear to ear. I hugged Harry and thanked him for all he had done. A moment later, I was in the taxi and headed off through the city toward the airport.

"We haven't much time," the driver said. "But I'll do my best to get you there by six."

We were halfway there before he realized that he had forgotten to put the meter on—and I realized that I had forgotten that taxis cost money. How was I going to pay the fare? I was so excited however, that I couldn't help but share what was happening with him. As it turned out, his North Shore route often took him to a place called Faith Center, a Christian Fellowship where we had received many blessings. He was very curious about what went on inside. I suggested that the next time he took a passenger there, he should park his taxi and find out for himself.

We arrived at the airport at two minutes to six.

I asked how much the fare was. He glanced at the meter, shrugged his shoulders and said, "Oh, a dollar will do."

That was only a fraction of the regular fare but I knew I might not even have that. I had given my last dollar to Harry. But I looked in my purse, just in case, and tucked away there was a one-dollar note. I paid him and hurried into the departure lounge.

Ray was already there, obviously wondering if I would make it or not. My brother, David, and my mother and father were also there to wave us off and give us something towards expenses. And just then, in walked Pam, carrying the cases. Following her were Nanna, Joy and Beth with the string bag of precious teddy bears.

It was 6 p.m. exactly. We were all there, not one minute late, glory be to God! The only thing left undone was the fact that Beth and Joy still had their navy school ribbons in their hair, but at a time like that, who cared?

The three of us boarded a plane for the first time in our lives, joyful and excited. We felt like royalty because God had made a way for us by His provision. As the plane took off, the thought that filled my mind was, *Truly, God is with us!*

Although I was exhausted, I was too excited to sleep. I just sat there and relived the events of the past few weeks, aware of a great sense of destiny. Without a doubt, this trip had all been planned and purposed by God. It wasn't the result of perfect and abiding faith in my part. It wasn't through my strength. I had felt weak and inadequate. I had failed. I had called the bank in a panic. It had seemed that God was showing me how much fear I had, rather than how much faith. Yet I knew I had to be obedient, no matter how I felt during the weeks of preparation and those final agonizing hours. I had to keep on towards the goal. Something deep inside me motivated me and propelled me forward. God's grace had covered my sin; He knew I was only beginning to learn His ways.

God had required me to be faithful in small things to discover His faithfulness in all things. I had struggled having to pick up the notices from the church office, but it was in the path of simple and seemingly unimportant duty that the Lord met me. God is faithful! If He gives us a commission or a command, we have only to set our will in motion with His and give Him the measure of faith that we have. Then, even when we seem to be overwhelmed with self and circumstances, He will not fail us.

It is God who chooses the time and the means. Sometimes we try to tell Him that the fulfillment of the promise should not be prolonged any more. We say in our frustration and impatience, "God, it's about time You did something!" But if there is a delay, it is only an opportunity to trust more in His wonderful love.

CHAPTER 12

I Will Do A New Thing

"Do not remember the former things, nor consider the things of old. Behold, I will do a new thing . . ."
Isaiah 43:18-19

While I was being tested and tried back home in Australia, Alan was in Los Angeles. He had been led of the Lord to go on a seven-day fast in regard to the children and me coming to America. He felt he should not try to contact me to see how I was doing, but rather to stand in faith and prayer for the family to join him in Los Angeles as planned. He met our plane at LA airport, not knowing if we were on it or not, but believing to see us among the passengers. It was wonderful to be together again, sharing how God had supplied the money for our tickets. With a great sense of anticipation we wondered what God would do next.

We were booked into a motel opposite Melodyland Christian Center in Anaheim, California, to attend the Annual Charismatic Clinic, and as Ray had nowhere to stay, we suggested he stay there with us. We settled in and tried to throw off jet lag with a good long rest. We woke in the middle of the night feeling hungry, and Ray went and spent his last few dollars on chicken.

The next morning we checked our financial situation. We had a grand total of $1.60, which was not going to stretch very far among three adults and two children. We did have plenty of free ice from the motel's ice machine. The motel also had a custard machine; 20 cents bought a small can. That satisfied the children temporarily, but by Sunday afternoon, all of us were hungry. There were no stores open nearby. The only cheap place to eat was the hot dog stand at Melodyland, just across the road. I took Beth and Joy and the remaining $1.40 and went to buy hot dogs. After that, we didn't know how we were going to eat.

Melodyland was just about deserted, and to our disappointment, the hot dog stand was closed. There went our last hope. Then it occurred to me that God had supplied hundreds of dollars for our fares to America. Now that we were here, He surely wouldn't let us starve. I realized that we had not even asked the Lord to supply the food we needed. Once again, He wanted us to depend on Him alone.

Taking Beth and Joy by the hand, I began to walk around the big deserted building that Joy always called a tent because of its round shape and pointed roof. I sang our promise out loud, "My God shall supply your every need, according to His riches…"

Beth and Joy were looking up at me strangely, but I encouraged them to believe God with me for our food. After all, there were enough examples in Scripture of miraculous provision of food. We kept on marching, right around the building. Nothing happened. But then, we really didn't know what we expected to happen.

We went back to the motel and told Alan what we had been doing. We had no choice but to wait for God to do something. In the meantime, we spent the precious remaining $1.40 on custard for Beth and Joy.

It wasn't long before Ray had some visitors, who just happened to give him ten dollars. Alan and I immediately thought of food—this had to be God's provision. Ray, however, thought differently. He felt he should keep it for his expenses later on. So we went on waiting and praying, and wondering if God thought the same thing as Ray.

A car drew up outside and a knock came on our door. An Australian voice called out, "Anybody home?"

"Why, it's David Reekes!" Alan exclaimed, clearly pleased to see his former traveling companion.

"I thought I would drop in and see how you're getting on," David explained. Then, after chatting for a few minutes, he came out with a marvelous suggestion. "Look, why don't you hop in the car? I'll drive you down to the supermarket and buy you some food."

Apparently Ray's idea had been God's idea after all.

Our first meal of bread and butter with bologna and cheese from an American supermarket tasted as good as if we were dining in Los Angeles' best restaurant. Better, in fact, because we were dining at the King's table, eating what He had so lovingly provided.

We came back from Melodyland the next day to find that a woman had left two large brown bags stuffed with food. Later that week, while we were crossing the parking lot, someone else leaned out his car window and called, "Could you use some meal tickets? We won't need them, and it's a shame to let them go to waste."

We never lacked for food the rest of the trip. This just proved to us that God would supply every need, but sometimes He waits for us to ask.

Not only did God teach us in very practical ways, He also expanded our vision through the places we visited and the people we met. This was especially true for Alan while on his round-the-world journey with David Reekes.

So far, Alan had found the trip to be exciting, exhilarating, and at times, extremely challenging. When he boarded the plane at Sydney airport and the doors were closed for take-off, Alan had a panic attack. His throat tightened, his heart pounded, and he found it difficult to breath. He felt desperate and wanted to get off the plane right away. Shocked, he realized that he was suffering from claustrophobia.

When he landed in Perth on the other side of Australia, he walked up and down in the transit lounge, praying in tongues and wanting to walk all the way back to Sydney. Knowing that he couldn't do that, and that he had committed himself to a trip right around the world, he realized that he had to face his fear of flying and go on with the journey.

The next stop was Singapore where, due to an electrical fault with the plane, they spent a night in a luxury hotel. It was a brief glimpse at Southeast Asia. Alan had no idea that just seven years later he would be back to speak at the World Summit Convocation.

On the following day they flew on to Israel where they stayed in the St. George Hotel in Jerusalem. This began a two-day visit to the Holy Land, hardly long enough to see it all, but enough to whet the appetite. Alan and David took a trip to Jericho, swam in the Dead Sea, and walked around Jerusalem. There were two places where Alan sensed a special presence of the Lord—the Garden Tomb and the Mount of Olives. It was a rich experience that left Alan with a love for "His land," and a sense that he would be back again.

Then it was on to Rome where they once again had a short couple of days to take in the wonderful sights, including the Coliseum and the catacombs where the early Christians met.

From there it was off to London and down to the University of Surrey in Guilford for The Fountain Trust Conference led by Reverend Michael Harper. This was the first major Charismatic conference ever held in Europe, and Alan felt like he was given a pressure-cooker exposure to what God was doing in this new move of the Spirit just beginning to go around the world. Major speakers included David DuPlessis, Ralph Wilkerson, Kevin Ranaghan, Arthur Wallis, David Watson, Dr. Rodman Williams, Robert Frost, and many others. Little did Alan realize that in the days to come he would be inviting many of the same speakers to minister in Australia.

The evening meetings were held in the nearby Anglican cathedral. It was the first time Alan had experienced a large gathering of believers worshipping in such a powerful way.

At the conference, Alan had a follow-up meeting with Anglican minister Ray Muller (whom he had met in Sydney) to discuss the vision of holding a national Charismatic conference in Sydney in January 1973, a week after a Ray's conference in New Zealand. Ray and Alan agreed to invite Michael Harper, Kevin Ranaghan, and Robert Frost to be the speakers.

While standing in a slow cafeteria line for dinner, Alan found himself talking to an older Pentecostal minister who shared with him the persecution that early Pentecostals had experienced, including open-air meetings where they had been pelted with rotten tomatoes. Alan gained a deep appreciation for the price that these Pentecostal pioneers had paid to proclaim the message of the Holy Spirit baptism.

After the conference, Alan and David spent some time in London, a city that they really liked. Alan was able to visit Central Hall where the great preacher William Sangster used to fill the pulpit. The sightseeing in historic London included visits to St. Paul's Cathedral, Westminster Abbey, Buckingham Palace, and Spurgeon's Temple, where a follow-up meeting to the Guilford Conference was held.

As he traveled on the Underground, Alan faced a challenging moment when the crowded train came to a halt under the Thames River. The lights went out. The fears of claustrophobia sought to return and Alan had to battle them off, standing on the promise of 1 Corinthians 10:13, that God does not allow us to tempted or tested above what we are able to bear.

Being a Methodist minister, it was only natural that Alan would find his way to some historic Methodist sights, including John Wesley's home. It was awe-inspiring to go into Wesley's room where he prayed and read his Bible every morning and night. The room was called "The Power House of Methodism."

Later, Alan visited Wesley's chapel that opened back in 1778. There he realized that, although grateful to God for his Methodist heritage, he was called to the whole Body of Christ, not just part of it. It was this revelation and call that would fashion his ministry in the years to come. As he stood in front of the statue of John Wesley, he read Wesley's words, "The world is my parish." Truly, this trip was expanding Alan's understanding of God's calling on our lives.

From London, Alan's next destination was New York and Teen Challenge, the original purpose of the trip. Once again, he had a challenging time on the airplane, but kept pressing into God for victory over claustrophobia. Arriving at Kennedy Airport, then on to Grand Central Station, Alan and David took a subway train to Clinton Avenue and from there walked to Teen Challenge.

It was a somewhat frightening experience to arrive in a completely different culture to anything Alan had known, and New York was not what he had imagined. He was told not to go out on the streets at night, as it was too dangerous. Alan and David stayed in an apartment building opposite the Teen Challenge Center, where they met Charles Ringma from Brisbane. Charles later became, for a time, the national director of Teen Challenge in Australia. They also met Don Wilkerson, David Wilkerson's brother, who was the director of Teen Challenge in New York at that time.

Sunday brought yet another new cultural experience when they attended a church in Harlem called the "Soul Saving Station for Every Nation." It was like no church service they had ever experienced, as the noisy service lasted 3 1/2 hours, considerably longer than what Alan was used to. Alan and David were the only white men in the church, but they were made very welcome. That night they went with the young men in the Teen Challenge program to another black church, this time in Queens. The preacher was terrific and Alan was now getting accustomed to the high level of congregational involvement. Indeed, Charles Ringma was with them, standing on his feet and shouting out, "Preach it, brother, preach it!"

On Monday they began the training seminar with participants from all over America. Teaching sessions were only a part of the seminar. The participants also visited a rescue mission and took part in outreaches to neighborhoods such as the Bowery, where Alan was saddened to see drunks lying all over the pavement - a sight that made a tremendous impact on him. On one such outreach, Alan had a 20-minute talk with a drug addict named Judy who had come from a good home, was married at age 13 to a man 15 years her senior, had her first child at 14, and now was a heroin addict at age 21. She knew she needed Jesus, but not just now.

Other visits included a Westchester Country prison, the Walter Hoving Home for Girls in upstate Garrison, and the Lost Coin Coffee Shop in Greenwich Village, run by David Wilkerson's mother, a quite remarkable lady.

On Saturday, Alan was unexpectedly asked to preach at the Teen Challenge chapel service. He spoke on Philippians 4:19, "My God will supply your every need." After the service, Alan prayed for a visiting student from Ashbury Methodist Seminary to receive the Baptism in the Holy Spirit.

The following week, Alan was baptized in water at the Teen Challenge Center by Don Wilkerson. While at seminary, through the writings of theologian Karl Barth, Alan had come to the conviction that believer's baptism was the New Testament model. However, having grown up in the Methodist church that preached infant baptism, he had never been baptized as an adult. (The previous summer, at my request, he had baptized me in the Pacific Ocean not far from our home in Waverly.) Before he had left Australia, he had the feeling that he would receive water baptism at Teen Challenge.

Teen Challenge usually held baptisms outside New York, at their farm in Pennsylvania. But that week they were holding a baptism for a group of ex-drug addicts from Greenwich Village, and Alan was able to join them. His experience was one of complete release, inner power and joy. He described it as "the rolling away of a burden off my back."

Undoubtedly, one of the great highlights of Alan's whole trip was a visit to Pittsburgh, Pennsylvania. With the assistance of Teen Challenge staff, David, Charles and Alan were able to attend a Kathryn Kuhlman service and were given front row seats in the packed First Presbyterian Church, for a service that lasted well over three hours.

This was mind-blowing for Alan. He had never experienced anything like this before. People were being healed in front of his eyes. Kathryn Kuhlman ministered with a word of knowledge, describing a specific illness, often in detail, and then asking people up to the platform to testify to the healing that had just occurred. Alan wept as he watched a woman walk who had not walked for three years, and a girl who had been healed of blindness on the bus going home from a previous meeting. There was the release of the power of the Holy Spirit as Miss Kuhlman prayed for people and they were "slain in the Spirit." He was impressed by Miss Kuhlman's declaration, "We vow by our lives to give You all the glory, Jesus." After the service, the three men spent the afternoon in a park opposite Three Rivers Stadium. Lying on the grass, they all agreed, "Isn't Jesus wonderful!"

From New York, Alan and David flew across the country to Houston, Texas to visit The Church of the Redeemer, led by Episcopal minister Graham Pulkingham. The church had formed a number of community households that ministered to troubled or needy people. They had the opportunity to experience this first hand as they stayed in one of the households. Alan was so impressed with the lifestyle of these people and their commitment to each other, that he felt we should start a community of our own back in Sydney. Finally, the time came to say goodbye to Texas and head for Los Angeles.

The week following our arrival in Los Angeles was a wonderful time of blessing for the family, now reunited after six weeks apart. Together we experienced the powerful Charismatic Clinic at Melodyland Christian Center. This was all so new to us, and we were inspired to hear such speakers as David Wilkerson, Dennis Bennett and Dick Mills. It was during this time that Beth had a beautiful experience of being baptized in the Spirit, receiving the gift of tongues.

At the end of the week, we said good-bye to our young friend, Ray, and headed north to Salem, Oregon, making stops at San Francisco and Seattle on the way. It was in Seattle that God brought deliverance for Alan from the spirit of rejection that had hung over his life for 36 years, even though he hadn't fully realized it.

Noel Bell had asked us to deliver a parcel to a friend of his in Seattle. The friend and her husband came to the hotel to pick it up. Naturally enough we invited them in to visit for a while. During our conversation, somehow or other the story of Alan's birth and his mother's rejection of him came up.

The woman, with great discernment, simply said, "Do you realize what that has done to you?"

Suddenly, Alan had a blinding revelation of how this rejection had affected him from his earliest childhood. His sense of inferiority, his lack of confidence, his poor self-image—all these had their roots in this spirit of rejection. Yes, we had known all the details of his birth, but now Alan realized what that had done to him. I joined the couple in laying hands on Alan, praying for him to be set free from the spirit of rejection that had been a cloud over his entire life.

That meeting in the hotel room in Seattle marked a major turning point for Alan. However, he also realized the need to not only "eliminate the negative," but also the importance of "accentuating the positive," to borrow the words of an old song. He had to develop a healthier self-image based upon who he was in Christ according to the word of God.

From Seattle we traveled on to Salem, Oregon, where World Map, directed by Ralph Mahoney, was holding a family camp. We found that God was saying the same thing there that He had been saying to us in Australia: *"Do not remember the former things, nor consider the things of old. Behold, I will do a new thing," (Isa 43:18-19).*

In Salem, Oregon, as the trip was drawing to a close, Alan looked back and saw all that God had done; the conferences, ministries, and churches he had visited, and the contacts with key leaders, many of whom would be invited to come and minister in Australia in the years ahead. He knew that although the initial purpose had been to study the work of Teen Challenge in New York, the larger purpose was to see the "new thing" God was doing in the Body of Christ in the Charismatic Renewal that would lay a foundation for the ministry that was about to be born in Australia. On top of that, Alan had been set free from a spirit of rejection. Truly, it was a God-ordained trip for each member of the family.

We felt that God had something special in store for us as we went home to Australia. Alan had been away nearly two months, and I had been away two weeks. In that time, God had enlarged us, stretched us, blessed us and spoken to us. We would never be the same again. God initiated the whole family into a way of life that was to become our daily walk from that time on. Truly, the former things were passing away. The security we had known, the ministry in the local church—that was all going to change.

We didn't know that then, of course. We thought this trip was a once in a lifetime experience. We certainly didn't anticipate that in just 12 months' time, we would be living through another real-life faith adventure. Perhaps it was just as well that we couldn't see that far ahead.

CHAPTER 13

A Taste of Community

"God sets the solitary in families."
Psalm 68:6

Our return from America in 1971 met with a cold reception from some church members. No one seemed overjoyed to welcome us back. Strangely enough, some of our closest, supportive friends hardly spoke to us. I caught the brunt of their hostility. After the first service back home, one woman refused to speak to me or shake my hand as we stood at the church door. Another confronted me in the hall and told me what she thought. "I think you were wrong in going to America," she said sternly. "You should have stayed at home." I was taken aback. We couldn't understand it. We decided to fast and pray for three days and seek the Lord.

To get to the bottom of the hostility, we called a meeting of the offended people at our home. We soon uncovered the misunderstanding. Alan had not informed the church that he had wanted me to join him in America and they thought I had decided to join him of my own accord. To the members of the church, it seemed as though I was doing it for my own enjoyment. Little did they know the agony I had been through the weeks before the trip. Praise the Lord, reconciliation began, and things settled back to normal

Life in the parsonage, however, was not that of a normal family. Before we went to America, God challenged us to take in a boarder. Peter, a young builder who was returning from the mission field needed accommodation for about six months. While Alan was making a request from the pulpit one Sunday, both he and I were convicted that we had two spare bedrooms in the parsonage and should take him in. After Peter left we were four again. We didn't intend to go looking for anyone else, but again God caught our attention.

One day, after a time of prayer in Alan's study, I felt a distinct prompting to go out for the local newspaper. The Lord assured me there was something in it He wanted me to read. The paper was folded over and tucked between the gate and the wall. Right on the fold of the newspaper I noticed an advertisement: "Quiet girl student wants accommodation in the Waverly area." As I read it, I knew that God wanted us to take her in. After prayer, both Alan and I felt we should call her. We found out the young lady, Carna, had already accepted an offer to move into a hostel, but when she heard what had happened she came for an interview with us. She was from Newcastle, straight from high school, pretty, petite, with long blonde hair. After tasting some homemade cookies she knew she was in the right place—only a few minutes walk from her college.

During Carna's three-year stay, she lived through all our ups and downs, trials, tribulations, joys and sorrows, as a special member of our extended family. She went through her own struggles, but through it all she gave her heart to the Lord and learned to trust Him.

After our trip to America, Ray came to live with us, so our family numbered six. Not for long, however. More were added, including Fred, who played the guitar for our meetings, and his friend Mark. Warwick, a young man who boarded next door, was a frequent visitor.

One of our most challenging guests was an ex-drug addict who came to us in 1972 and stayed a few months. A pastor from Newcastle had asked if we would take him in, knowing Alan was interested in a Teen Challenge-type ministry. Jim was a tall, middle-aged man, and before he joined us, had just experienced a dramatic conversion, baptism in the Spirit and deliverance from drugs.

Jim was a mixture. We found him a sensitive, loving man, yet unwilling to totally follow the Lord. He had the esteemed position of guru, a wise man and a father figure in the drug counter-culture. His wisdom was sometimes spiritual, but often of the world and the flesh. A man with great potential to be a disciple of Christ, yet he followed only part of the way. Christianity, he declared, was too hard, too costly. He was not prepared to give up his free-sex life, nor did he think that others should have any restrictions imposed on them. He wasn't prepared to let the Lord deal with every area of his life and put his choices and lifestyle under the Lordship of Jesus Christ.

Late one evening, I was horrified to hear a sample of his worldly counsel in conversation he was having with Warwick from next door while sitting on our back terrace. He said, "If you want sex, it's just as easy as eating a banana, just pick it up and peel it any time you want." I was furious with Jim for still holding fast to his foolish ways, as well as trying to influence someone else.

Having Jim in the house was unpredictable. At dinner one evening, he picked up his knife and threatened Ray with it. Beth, Joy and I were the only others there. Alan was away so we were thankful when Jim controlled his anger and decided not to use the knife.

He did good work as a carpenter for one of the local ministers, but he couldn't break with old ways. He left us and went back to his old scene of drugs and sex. We found him one day half-a-mile from our home in an empty rented house that had been vacated by one of our friends. Jim was on the floor, cowering like a little dog in the corner. He wouldn't come back with us. We don't know what became of him after that.

Times were not always dramatic or traumatic for the occupants of Number 12 Leichhardt Street. Sometimes we just had fun. Alan and Fred would often wrestle one another and resort to pulling hairs on each other's legs, or putting on strangleholds and faking choking by holding their breath and going red in the face. This would always bring me to the rescue, beating them both with a rolled up newspaper, the only way to restore order. We had sock fights, with shaving cream for extra ammunition. On one occasion, Alan tricked Ray by asking him to go around to the side of the house to pick up something under the bathroom window. Alan was waiting with a bucket of water balanced on the windowsill. At the opportune moment he tipped it all over Ray.

For Beth, our eldest daughter, this was great fun. The young men and women were just like older brothers and sisters. The variety of different people and activities proved quite an education—not the kind one would receive in school.

For Joy, the circumstances were a little more difficult. She wasn't at school and so she missed Beth a great deal. At times she would sit in a chair with her "bunny-rug" (her baby blanket) and rock herself. We would do things together in the day. Then in the evening there was always so many people we didn't have time to be a normal family. On one occasion, I asked Joy why she was so sad, and she said, "Everyone is so big and I'm the only little one."

When the household was too hectic, she and Beth would withdraw to the playroom and lose themselves playing with dolls or in pretending they were in school. She longed to have someone her own age to play with, but there were no other playmates in our vicinity, so we arranged for her to attend St. Catherine's Church of England Kindergarten. This eventually proved to be very beneficial for her. Her teacher was wonderful and she found good friends there.

It was no wonder Joy felt outnumbered. We had people staying in every available space, even in the garage. Our typical evening meal would number between 10 to 12, apart from visitors. Running the household was quite a challenge. The grocery shopping for such a big number was gigantic. The preparation of the meals and cleanup was a huge task also, even though everyone was required to help.

This taste of community was a learning experience for us and also for an associated household led by friends Bruce and Judy Warren. Bruce later became one of Alan's administrators.

Although I enjoyed community life and felt God wanted us involved in that particular lifestyle, it was also a big responsibility. There were times when I felt completely inadequate for the situation. I was continually faced with opportunities to cry out to God for wisdom and strength, learning that His grace was sufficient for my every need. We found out a lot of things that community should not be. We learned by our mistakes. The foundational mistake was that we lacked the proper understanding about community living in such critical issues as leadership and headship, which this lifestyle demands.

Although people loved living together, the level of maturity varied considerably from one person to another, each with different expectations of what a community lifestyle meant. After Alan had been to the Church of the Redeemer in Houston, Texas, and had seen their community households, he had come back and wanted to do the same thing. We found out that it is one thing to see what God is doing somewhere else and another thing to understand the principles, to go through the preparation, and to pay the price. We rushed into community life when we weren't ready for it.

We realized that we were not experienced enough, nor mature enough to give solid leadership to the group in the household. Alan was not able to handle the demands that such a situation required in addition to all the other things he was doing in the ministry.

Clockwise starting above –
Dorothy's Family, Dorothy as a child,
Dorothy's older brother Alan who died at the
age of 13, Dorothy's Family on the
Promenade in Wales, Dorothy's parents
Walter and Mary Roan.

Clockwise starting top –

Alan with his parents William and Catherine
Langstaff on his 21st Birthday,
Alan graduating in Architecture,
Alan in a school photo,
The Langstaff Boys – Alan's Father and
his two older brothers George and Ken,
Alan playing soccer.

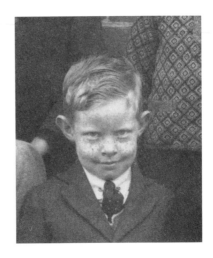

Clockwise starting above –

Dorothy and her
Sunday School Class at
Moorfields Methodist Church,
Dorothy at 17 years of age,
Dorothy (back row) as a prefect at
Fort Street Girls High School,
Dorothy and her Family –
Dorothy, brother John, mother,
brother David and father.

Clockwise starting above –
Alan and Dorothy on their
wedding day in 1958, Beth (6), Joy (4), Alan and
Dorothy at the Architects Ball, Alan and Dorothy's
first house designed by Alan
(Inset – garage where they first lived).

Clockwise starting above left –

Lugar Brae Parsonage, Home on Bronte Road, Lugar Brae Church

Clockwise starting above –

Temple Trust Staff,
Alan and Dorothy in 1979,
First Temple Trust Office
(small office on right side of building),
Last Temple Trust Office
in Leyland House on the Top Floor.

Clockwise starting above –

Conference in 1977 in Sydney,
Jim Spillman ministering
at the 1976 Conference,
Ralph Wilkerson preaching at the
1974 Conference in Canberra,
Roman Catholic Father Francis
McNutt and Protestant Tommy
Tyson praying for forgiveness and
reconciliation at the 1977
Conference in Sydney.

Clockwise starting above –
Alan interviewing Oral Roberts on the
Australian PTL Club, Alan and
Dorothy first met Jim Bakker on the
PTL Club at Heritage USA, Alan
preaching with Dr. Cho interpreting.

Clockwise starting above – Hebron (1989), an old Victorian Mansion, home of Vision Bible College. Joy and Cindy, Alan and Dorothy at the opening of Vision Bible College, First intake of Bible College Students, Langstaff Family.

Clockwise starting top –
Jesus 79' – Opening Service at
Opera House, Opening
Service, Crowds at Randwick
Racecourse, 'New Day' at The
Gap, Alan preaching 'New
Day' message.

THE TIME OF TESTING

CHAPTER 14

Delay Is Not Denial

"For the vision is yet for an appointed time;
but at the end it will speak and it will not lie.
Though it tarries wait for it; because it will surely
come, it will not tarry."
Habakkuk 2:3

"People are coming from all over the world to the 1972 Olympic Games in Munich," declared Dean Sherman, Australian director of Youth With A Mission (YWAM). He had the full attention of the local charismatic leaders who were meeting in our living room.

"Authorities predict that it will be the largest international gathering in the history of the Games," Dean continued. "YWAM plans to seize this great opportunity for evangelism. We have sent out a call for young Christians around the world to come to the city of Munich and let the world know that Jesus is Lord."

It certainly sounded exciting! Having just returned from one major overseas trip, I had no thoughts of going on another one. Alan, however, felt a witness in his spirit that he was to go and take a group with him. As he prayed and sought the Lord, the conviction became stronger. "Yes," he said. "I'm sure that God wants me to go and I think you should pray about going too."

Another trip so soon? Hesitatingly, I went to my room and knelt beside my bed. If I were to go on another adventure, the Lord would have to convince me that it was His will. I prayed with The Living Bible in front of me and was led to a passage from Isaiah chapter 13, beginning at verse 2: *"See the flags waving...shout to them, O Israel, and wave them on as they march...I the Lord have set apart these armies for this task. I have called those rejoicing in their strength to do this work. Hear the tumult and shout of many nations. The Lord of Hosts has brought them here from countries far away."*

"This is amazing, Lord!" I cried. "The verses I'm reading sound like a description of an international gathering. Maybe You do want me to go to Munich."

I opened my King James version to the same passage and verses 7 and 8 caught my attention. *"And every man's heart shall melt and they shall be afraid. Pangs and sorrows shall take hold of them."* The "shouts of many nations with their flags waving" made sense, but the verse about "pangs and sorrows" left me puzzled.

The more I prayed and thought about the decision, the more convinced I became that the Lord wanted us to go to Munich as a family.

We weren't the only ones who felt a call to go. Richard Wills, our Christian real estate agent, was thrilled to hear of the YWAM outreach. He had dreamt about a castle filled with young people. YWAM, we found out, had acquired a castle in the little village of Hurlach, 40 miles from Munich, to house the hundreds of young people who were coming to witness at the Olympic Games. Richard made plans to go, as did a number of others, including Fred, Mark and Kevin, three young men who had recently joined our household. Ray had a different call this time: to stay and take care of things and feed our pets.

It seemed sensible to organize a tour group to Munich, and for Alan to lead it. Planning began with the help of our travel agent, Harry Hollister. We would leave on August 8, fly to Singapore for a day or two, spend a week in Israel and on to Munich for training and outreach. After that, the members of the tour could go their separate ways. As a family, we planned to go to Britain, visit my Auntie Jean in Wales where I had been born, and then go up to Carlisle to see my Uncle John. How exciting that would be, to see people and places I hadn't seen since I was a little girl. To have Alan, 11-year-old Beth and five-year-old Joy with me would add an extra blessing.

Alan asked the church for a leave of absence. The elders were a little concerned. The Superintendent minister was away on a long overseas trip so they were placed in a difficult situation. They gave their reluctant permission and we agreed not to receive any salary during Alan's absence.

The seven of us in the parsonage began believing for our fares. On the basis of the conviction that God wanted us to go to Munich and had proven Himself faithful in previous experiences, Alan and I waited on God's provision now with much less trauma. It seemed only yesterday that we had been believing to go to America. God had kept me waiting until the last day before all the money was provided and we were willing to wait until the last day again. We had no doubt that God would supply. I'm not sure that the others shared our confidence, but they prayed and waited along with us. Alan felt that even if God didn't give Fred, Mark and Kevin all they needed, he would send enough to Alan to cover their expenses.

The initial money came in an unexpected way. Some years before, Alan's Auntie Meg, who had never married and who owned a women's clothing store in Kempsey, NSW, had died and her estate had been distributed to six of her relatives, including Alan. Now, out of nowhere, we received a phone call from her bank manager saying that they had found another one of her accounts with three to four thousand dollars in it. Again, this was distributed among the relatives and Alan received enough to pay his whole airfare. However, instead of paying for his own, he used it as deposits for all of us.

It didn't seem strange to us that the money came in slowly. God is sometimes slower than we like Him to be. Undaunted, we prepared for the trip. We packed our clothes and organized replacements for Alan in the church services. We were ready except for one thing—seven people were believing to go and Alan only had enough money for one.

Up to that point, when money had come in, he had spread it out evenly towards the cost of seven tickets. Now, on the eve of departure, he sat at his desk and looked honestly at the situation. He started to get an uneasy feeling in the pit of his stomach. His plan hadn't worked out as expected. In a matter of hours, we were due to leave with the tour group led by Alan. We prayed and talked and prayed. Alan and I decided that we had to follow through. We would all go out to the airport, complete with luggage, expecting God to supply the money somehow.

The next day, Ray drove all seven of us, with varying degrees of faith, out to the airport. A large number of people were already gathered. Dean Sherman was there, as well as Paul Collins from Faith Center. The tour group was waiting excitedly, talking to the friends and relatives who had come to wish them well.

It was time to board the plane and nothing happened. A girl's voice announced our flight over the loudspeaker and asked the passengers to board. Alan gave a hurried explanation to the tour and suggested they board the plane. All we could do was pray and wait until time ran out.

The moment of truth came about half an hour later when we heard the final boarding call. With a sinking feeling, we realized that God was not going to perform a miracle. We didn't know what to do. The plane was taking off with the tour on its way to Singapore without Alan, the tour leader, on board. We stood, dazed, trying to explain to those who had come to see us off why we were still there. They must have been very confused and alarmed.

It was a subdued group that picked up their heavy bags and slowly followed Alan out to the van. Alan tried to cheer us up by suggesting that we all go out to dinner. We were all disappointed and puzzled and wrestled with our emotions. Some responded in frustration and anger. Our faith was certainly being tested. After a cup of tea back home, we gathered in the living room to talk and pray. Alan explained that there was only enough money for one fare. As he talked, I knew he would have to use that money to go and join the others as soon as possible. A wonderful peace and calm filled my heart. I knew God would work things out.

Alan went into his study. Ray, sensing his dilemma, joined him there. They knelt at the old green armchairs and prayed. Alan began to weep brokenly, crying out to God, "All these people...I'm supposed to be their leader—half of them gone on the plane and half of them still here. What am I going to do, Lord?"

Even as he was weeping and praying and even as he asked the question, he knew the only answer. At the airport, Dean

Sherman and Paul Collins had talked with Alan about the financial situation. They had pointed out that God had provided the money for him to go, and since he had committed himself to lead the group, he should follow through with that commitment. Alan had realized that they were right. He would have to use the money he had received himself and get on the first available flight to join the others.

It was agony for him to think of leaving the girls and me behind when we had believed and planned to go together. It was made more painful by the fact that he was leaving me without any salary. His grief and pain were obvious as he stood in the hall outside the study and, in tears, tried to tell me what I already knew. He would have to go. I tried to reassure him that God was in control, even if we couldn't understand. We still believed that the girls and I were meant to go to Munich.

Alan called to see if there were any seats on flights to Singapore. The airline called back. Yes, there was one cancellation on a BOAC flight leaving the next morning. He booked it. Then, soberly, he broke the news to the household. Everyone agreed it was the only thing he could do. One young man decided to stay home. The other two later raised their fare money and joined the tour in Israel a few days later.

I was so sure that God wanted me and the children to go, and so convinced that he would make a way possible, that I decided to go out to the airport again with Alan. God still had time to perform a mighty miracle and I wasn't going to miss it by staying home. Ray offered to drive us out to the airport. The rest of the household, not sure I was acting sensibly, comforted themselves that I could soon be back home without Alan and they would have a cup of tea and sympathy ready for me.

There was no big crowd at the airport this time. Ray, Dean Sherman and one of his workers were the only ones there. Alan began the procedure for departure. For the girls and I to go, there would have to be three more seats and the money to pay for them. We were expecting anything to happen, right up to the last minute. Then the voice came over the loudspeaker announcing his flight. We both knew Alan had to go this time, and there was a deep ache in our hearts as we realized that God had not opened the way for the girls and I to go. We didn't understand. We had been obedient to God, stepped out in faith expecting the Red Sea to part in front of us. But it hadn't.

Saying goodbye was traumatic, and yet God gave us the grace to be brave. Alan left us feeling as though his heart was being torn in two. He turned to wave as he went through the opening in the frosted glass partition and I could see the agony on his face as he looked toward me. As he disappeared, a horrible emptiness and loneliness enveloped me. I looked at Ray. He didn't say much. Perhaps he was wondering what I was going to do next. He smiled with relief when I suggested we all go back home. I didn't feel I could prolong the agony for Beth, Joy or myself.

Alan was sitting in the plane somewhere on the tarmac as Ray turned the van towards home and started down the freeway. I couldn't help but remember the last trip to America and the exciting dash to the airport along the same freeway. I had been scared that God wouldn't provide the money in time, but He had. This time, I had been confident He would provide money, but He hadn't. I just couldn't understand. I watched the wire mesh fence enclosing the airport grounds merge into a blur as the speed of the van increased. Beyond the fence there were so many planes, all sizes and colors. A large jet was moving slowly along the runway, ready for takeoff. Was it Alan's? I felt guilty that I had not stayed to wave the plane off. But that would have been too heartbreaking. I just wanted to leave the scene as soon as possible.

We were sitting quietly in the van, too sad to talk, when Ray blurted out, "I feel sick. We'll have to stop somewhere." We were on the freeway with nowhere to pull over. "We'll have to go back to the airport. I have to find a bathroom," he said urgently.

There was a break in the center island just ahead of us, so we turned back to the airport. I knew then we had to go and see Alan's plane off. While Ray headed for the closest bathroom, Beth, Joy and I ran out on the observation deck to find Alan's plane. There were so many planes I didn't know where to look. I remembered seeing the big jet on the runway that might have been the BOAC. Excited, Joy pulled on my hand "Look, Mummy, look at that stripy plane down there."

I glanced at the plane she was pointing to and saw that it was a KLM Royal Dutch Airlines plane. I could have been on that KLM plane, I thought miserably. My brother worked for Qantas and his close relatives could fly certain airlines on concession rates. But I put that thought out of my mind. It wasn't much good to me now. Besides, I was concerned about finding a BOAC jet.

We ran across the other side of the deck, and scanned the tarmac. Yes! There it was, out on the runway, waiting for the signal to take off. We watched the huge plane begin to move and gather speed. Then, as if pulled up by an invisible chain, it left the ground and flew off directly away from us. It shrank to the size of a great bird and Beth and Joy stood on tiptoe to watch it get smaller and smaller. We would wait until it vanished from sight.

Right in front of us, a little red-haired boy was sitting on a man's shoulders. He turned and said excitedly to me, "It's David, it's David!" pointing to the disappearing plane. As he spoke, my heart leapt within me. It was as though the Lord himself had spoken to me, showing me how I would be able to join Alan in Munich. David was the name of my brother who worked for Qantas. Through little Joy, the Lord had already turned my attention to KLM. That was it, of course! Why hadn't I thought of it before? I would ask David to arrange a concession ticket for me, at a cost of $200 instead of $700. I was sure the Lord would supply the money for it and for the children's half fares. Back home, everyone was waiting to comfort me. They expected a long, sad face, but I arrived home elated. I told them how God had just spoken to me and told me what to do. They listened without enthusiasm. They probably thought I was clutching at straws. I knew I had hold of something much more substantial than straws! I had hold of God, and His word to me! I called my brother, David, and shared my inspiration. "Is it possible to get a concession ticket on KLM?" I asked.

There was a pause. "Well, yes, normally you could get a concession ticket." he said. "But I'm afraid there's a dispute between KLM and Qantas at the moment, and the ticket writers are on strike. They won't write staff concession tickets."

"Oh, no," I groaned. "How long will it last?"

David said it could be several weeks.

"Perhaps if you explain my plight, they'll make an exception."

"Perhaps," said David. "I'll do what I can. They're having a meeting this Wednesday to try and settle that dispute."

"There is hope, then," I said.

David promised to call me about one o'clock on Wednesday with the decision. Meanwhile, we would wait and pray. I felt it was important to keep our cases packed, ready to go at a moment's notice. The Lord had given me a passage of scripture about having favor with those in authority, and that they would grant our request. I was sure it applied to our present circumstances.

Wednesday came. Ray was standing by to take us to the airport again. Our cases were closed. We were dressed to go. The girls had their teddy bears and airline bags ready. We waited in the dining room for the phone call. The phone rang.

It was my brother's voice.

"What's the news, David?" I asked.

"I'm terribly sorry," he said with genuine concern, "but the strike is still on. I explained your situation, but they won't make out a concession ticket until September 6."

He must have sensed my disappointment, even though I tried to be brave about it. I felt as though the bottom had dropped out of my world. By now, the girls realized what was happening. Beth looked at me anxiously. "What's wrong? Can't we go now?"

I explained, holding back my tears. Beth ran crying to her room. Dear little Joy walked through the house saying, "I don't care when I go as long as I go."

Ray looked me straight in the eyes and said firmly, "Why don't you just accept the fact that God doesn't want you to go?"

With that remark ringing in my ears, I fled to Alan's study, threw myself down in the chair behind the desk, put my head on my arms and sobbed my heart out. It would be easier to believe it had all been a mistake. But I couldn't believe that even if I wanted to. I knew God had said we were to go to Munich. I had no peace to let go of the whole idea, and yet I didn't know what to do. I felt so helpless. It seemed that everything was working against it. No matter what I did, the doors closed in my face. There weren't any words to describe the agony I felt. I could only cry out, "Oh God! Oh, God! I don't understand!"

Mingled with the sound of my own sobbing, I could hear Beth's muffled cries as she lay face down on the bed. I grieved for the frustration, hurt and disappointment she must be feeling. I didn't know how to comfort her. I was so overwhelmed myself. How could I ask my children to do the impossible when it was tearing them apart?

"God, I can't go through this again. I can't put my children through this agony."

I sat there in Alan's study, in turmoil, with the ache in my heart more than I could bear. I felt the spirit of God stirring in the depths of my being, rising up slowly, so slowly, through all the confusion and agony. I seemed to hear the quiet voice of the Lord asking, "Would you be willing to be ready to go? Would you be willing to tell Beth and Joy that they have to be ready one more time?"

I wanted to cry out, "No, I can't!" But God's Spirit was at work, making me willing and able to do His will.

"Oh God, it's so hard. If You want me to tell Beth and Joy that they have to be ready again, if you want me to be ready, believing to go some time in the future, then I need encouragement for my faith; not just to put myself through the agony, but to put my children through it, too."

It was agony for me to know that particularly Beth was suffering so greatly, and yet I could not alleviate her suffering. "I have tried to obey You, but the circumstances are a contradiction to everything You have said."

I reached for a book on Alan's desk, *Hinds Feet on High Places*, and opened it at random. The first words I read were, *"It is not contradiction, only postponement, for the best to become possible."* [1]

My heart skipped a beat. Awed, I realized that God was talking directly to me. I sensed the Lord's presence permeating the room and me. I glanced at the page again, hesitant for fear of losing that presence. The words leapt up! *"Much-Afraid, do you love Me enough to accept the postponement and the apparent contradiction of the promise, and to go down there with Me into the desert?"* [2]

I whispered, "Yes Lord," my voice barely audible in the stillness.

Even if I didn't understand, my desire was to trust God. I was willing to do whatever He wanted. Now I knew without a shadow of a doubt that it was His will for me to go to Munich. With that assurance, I could endure the delay with fresh faith and determination, knowing that the delay was in His will.

When the awesome feeling of God's presence faded, I was faced with the reality of my own weakness, but praise God, I had His words recorded on the page in front of me. I read on intently. The chapter was entitled, "The Detour through the Desert." The Shepherd had promised to take a crippled girl called Much-Afraid up to the High Places, and had chosen Sorrow and Suffering for her companions. Abruptly, the path had turned away from the High Places and led into the desert. In imagery, her experience was just what I was going through. The High Places represented Munich, and the desert was the place of waiting. Much-Afraid's words echoed my thoughts.

"You mean," she said incredulously, ". . . it is indefinite postponement?"

He was leading her away from her heart's desire altogether, and gave her no promise at all as to when He would bring her back. [3]

When asked if she would accept the postponement, her answer became the prayer of my heart.

"I do love You. . . . Even if You cannot tell me why it has to be, I will go with You. . . . You have the right to choose for me anything that You please." [4]

As I was meditating on that, I became aware again of Beth's quiet sobs. I knew I had to go and tell her how the Lord had spoken to me through the story of Much-Afraid. I prayed for the strength and wisdom to tell her. I went into her room and sat next to her on the bed.

I began to reassure her that God had not broken His word. Even though there was a delay and everything looked wrong, He still wanted us to join Daddy in Munich. He was asking us to be ready one more time. I read to her the passage from *Hind's Feet on High Places* and prayed that God would comfort her and strengthen her faith. My heart ached for her. I was hoping the story of Much-Afraid would speak to her as it had spoken to me, but there was no positive response. She was too upset to accept it then.

At the time, I didn't realize that she was angry and resentful, as well as disappointed. She had seen God provide for us the previous year and believed He would again. She had made a countdown chart, marking down each week and day until the proposed date of departure. She had told all her school friends that she was going to the Olympic Games. She had even given her birthday money towards the trip. To walk into her father's study and put her $13 on his desk was one of the hardest things she had ever done. She had never possessed so much money. Now it seemed that God had taken her money and was giving her a nice little story about someone called Much-Afraid instead. It wasn't fair. How would she ever face her school friends again? I kept the girls off school while we waited for the strike to end, but that didn't alleviate her fears.

She met a school friend while she was out shopping and had to give an embarrassed explanation. She was worried that everyone at school would find out.

God was allowing Beth to go through her own test of faith. The previous year, she had been shielded from the trauma and testing, but not this year. She had to learn a little more patience. She learned that things don't always happen when we think they should. God's timing is not always ours. That lesson was invaluable, as she had a tendency to be impatient wanting to run ahead of God. It was a hard lesson for an eleven-year-old, but God knew what He was doing.

Both Beth and I were learning that delay was not denial, only a postponement for the best to become possible. If God makes a promise, then we must wait in faith and patience for Him to make it good. Even if it looked too late, we must wait for God to act, accepting the apparent denial of His promise, even when we didn't understand.

Alan called from Jerusalem that evening. The connection was dreadful. Every word we spoke was echoed back. It was worse than four people all talking at once and made it almost impossible to communicate. I burst into tears of frustration. I tried to tell Alan what had happened and he tried to encourage me. Aware that I had no money, he told me to sell his golf clubs and stamp collection if I needed to. We could also cash in two small insurance policies. Perhaps the Lord wanted us to finance some of the trip this way.

I began making inquiries the next day. The insurance office was helpful, but with all the red tape, it was unlikely that the cash would be available in time. I filled out the necessary forms anyway. I began searching the want ads for anyone interested in second-hand golf clubs or stamp and coin collections.

I contacted Harry, our travel agent, and explained my circumstance. I booked three seats on KLM for September 6. David arranged for me to acquire my concession ticket as soon as possible after the strike ended.

The next few weeks were a real test of my faith. I had to search every drawer, box and tin in the house to find enough money to buy a loaf of bread. I gained new appreciation for the value of one cent. One day, I planned to make chow mein and fried rice for the evening meal. I needed some celery, but even half a bunch was too expensive. I only had eight cents left. In the green grocers, I noticed a few sticks of celery. I asked the price, and I was delighted when the woman answered, "You can have them for eight cents." The Lord showed His love for me even in the tiny details of day-by-day living.

I told my parents about my plans. "Well, I'll say one thing for you," my mother said with admiration, "you certainly are tenacious." She offered to lend me the money I needed until the insurance policy came through. We agreed to meet for lunch in town. I stopped at the insurance office on the way to see if my money was there, unlikely though that was. I made my way to the inquiry counter. The woman was pleasant and sympathetic and went to find out. She came hurrying back. "Well, this is most unusual," she said, "but your application is through. I've never known it to happen so fast. All you need to do is take this claim form, go to the banker, and he will give you the money." At lunch, I was able to tell Mum that I had the money and didn't need her loan.

I added that money to the proceeds from the sale of Alan's golf clubs, stamp and coin collection, and the money I had received previously. It was enough. Praise the Lord, I wouldn't have to wait until the last day to buy the girls' tickets and I was able to tell David I had the $200 for my concession ticket.

With Harry's help, we booked flights to Zurich, Switzerland. After a six-hour stopover there, we would fly SwissAir to Munich to meet Alan. As things began to work out, we started to get excited again. Unless the strike ended earlier, we would be ready to go on September 6. All we had to do was wait.

CHAPTER 15

Giving Up Your Rights

"Whoever desires to come after me, let him deny himself and take up his cross and follow Me."
Mark 8:34

Alan, meanwhile, was going through his own testing time after saying goodbye to us at the Sydney Airport. When he boarded the BOAC flight, he found he had a window seat, so he swapped it for one on the aisle. He felt bad enough leaving the family without the added trauma of claustrophobia. While the plane refueled at Perth, he wandered up and down the airport in a state of agitation, praying in the Spirit. He eventually fell asleep on the plane, only to wake with a start, troubled about me and the children back home.

In Singapore, he joined up with the rest of the tour, much to their relief. Then it was off to Israel. On arrival at Tel Aviv, they were taken out into a field and searched. The security was very strict. Even though he felt ready to cave in, Alan struggled through all the procedures of banking, baggage and forward bookings, as well as his other responsibilities as tour leader. On the bus ride to Jerusalem, he asked the Lord again the reason for his separation from the family. It would help if he knew what God was doing. But still no understanding came.

The visit to the Holy Land was a memorable one, and God obviously was blessing the little group. Initially, they stayed at the Mt. Scopus Hotel, and later at a Catholic pilgrim house on the Mount of Olives called Mission d'Abraham, where they received free room and board. What a glorious view it was to wake up in the morning and look across at the shining city of Jerusalem.

As all tourists do, they took in the sites around the Holy City. On Sunday they attended a wonderful service at the Garden Tomb where Merv and Merla Watson contributed the special music. On Tuesday, the group was joined by Fred and Kevin, who delivered a letter from me. Alan was thrilled to receive it, but during a later phone call, he realized that I was under great strain not knowing quite what to do.

Alan was constantly reminded of his family back home throughout his time in Israel. He woke up thinking of us. He spent much time seeking the Lord on our behalf, believing that we would still join him, if not in Israel, then in Munich.

The last two nights were spent in a hotel in Tel Aviv. The water of the Mediterranean was beautiful and warm when they went for a swim. It was there that they baptized Jennifer, one of the group who wanted to be baptized in the Holy Land. Later, they watched a beautiful sunset as the sun slipped into the ocean.

The tour group arrived in Munich and was taken to the YWAM headquarters in the village of Hurlach. Alan met with a few shocks on arrival. First, he discovered that his name had been left off their list and so YWAM wasn't even expecting him. Normally, they would have put a minister in charge of a group. Alan, however, was tacked on to a group of New

Zealanders, separated from the Australians. His team leader was a woman. The accommodation was another shock.

A castle sounded like luxury, but this castle was meant to house a maximum of 200 people. YWAM crammed in 900. Alan's bedroom was the fourth-floor attic, 101 steps up. He was given a six-by-three foot slot on a long wooden platform for his airbed, sleeping bag, and belongings. At night, a row of bodies slept on his left and right, with more rows on the platforms above. He took some time getting used to these conditions.

The bathrooms were as crowded as the bedrooms, so it was arranged that people would be bussed in the afternoon to a local bathing pool where they could have hot showers. Unfortunately, Alan was on work duty in the printing shop and missed out. He ended up going with a few of the Australian team once a week to a local river a mile or so away to bathe and wash clothes.

Alan had time for long walks in the countryside, prayer and devotions when he had finished work duty in the printing shop, and attended lectures in the big meeting tent. The messages were excellent. Speakers included Loren Cunningham, Joy Dawson, Brother Andrew, Corrie Ten Boom, and Vic Ramsey.

For Alan, the most memorable message was given by Loren Cunningham on the subject, "Giving up your Rights." Loren preached from Philippians 2. Jesus had to give up His rights and privileges, he said, and if we wanted to follow Him, God would ask us to give up our rights. Loren put his message into an equation: "Responsibility minus Rights equals Rewards and Privileges in the Kingdom of God."

That message spoke straight to Alan's heart. It explained what God was doing. He recalled how the previous year God had given us a promise and a vision of ministering together. This year, God was asking Alan to give back the very thing He had given—the right to have his family with him. Not only had God separated him from his family, but He had stripped Alan of any rights and privileges as a minister. Everything that was part of normal life—wife, family, ministry, bed, bath, privacy—had been taken from him.

The next day Alan went for a walk to think over what God had said. His walk took him through the village and past the cemetery. Previously, Alan had exercised leadership and responsibility. Now, in Germany, God had brought him low and asked him to give up all his rights, especially his wife and family. He had the humbling experience of becoming a nobody.

Alan cried out to the Lord, "I am nothing, I am nothing!"

He confessed his unworthiness, his pride and his sin. He walked to the crematorium chapel, intending to stay there until the Lord finished the death of self in him. But the doors were locked. Then the Lord spoke two words, as clear as an audible voice: "Tis done!"

God had done His work. Alan walked around the cemetery, praising Him. Release flowed from that time on. Soon afterwards, Alan received word that the girls and I would be coming on September 6, in approximately 14 days.

There was plenty to keep him busy while he waited. The following day was the first day of outreach at the Olympic Games. For the next three weeks, the teams would spend one day at the castle, the next day witnessing in Munich.

Alan was thrilled when one of the first people he witnessed to, a German boy, came to the Lord. It wasn't always that easy. He didn't see fruit from his witnessing every time. As he wrote in his diary, "I realized that there was pride in my heart. All the time I was anxious for God to be working through me. God wanted me to rejoice in what He was doing through others. If revival came, and I had no part in it, should I rejoice like the angels in heaven? I confessed my pride, and in faith I claimed the power to rejoice in what the Lord was doing."

On September 2, the YWAMers planned a rally. Their Jesus festival would begin with a march to the Olympic Stadium. The police, afraid of a riot, brought the march to a halt. The Christian young people were allowed to go, but only in small groups.

At one of the morning services, Loren Cunningham took up an offering towards the purchase of the castle after testifying how God had led them to this property. He challenged people with two questions: Are you to give? And if so, how much? Alan felt God tell him to give all that he had, even though it wasn't very much, including his spare change.

Alan spent much time thinking and praying about me. Although he would have loved me to be with him, he realized how difficult the schedule and lifestyle would have been for me with two small children. He had to content himself with letters. As the arrival date drew near, he decided to fast and pray during the time I would be on the flight.

On the day of our departure from Sydney, the Lord woke him at 4 a.m., exactly 1 p.m. Sydney time. My KLM plane was just taking off. The journey was an exciting one for me. God had supplied our needs and in His own time had kept His word that Alan and I would be together in Munich. As I sat in the plane approaching the Karachi airport, I had a quiet confidence of being right in the center of God's will. It was raining heavily when we landed, and the ground crew scuttled around in long yellow raincoats. There must have been trouble at the airport, because the plane had to stay out on the tarmac and no one was allowed to leave the plane. One man was allowed on board to sell newspapers. He came in dripping water from his long yellow coat and cap. I bought a paper, though I had little interest in newspapers normally. I thought it might help pass the time.

The whole front page was one bold black headline: MURDER IN MUNICH. Horrified, I read how Palestinian terrorists from Black September had taken Israeli athletes hostage at the Olympic village and had massacred 11 of them. "Oh, God, how terrible," I exclaimed under my breath, hardly able to believe what I was reading. Munich and its millions had been plunged into grief. Then I recalled the scripture that God had given me months before from Isaiah 13: *"...every man's heart shall melt and they shall be afraid. Pangs and sorrows shall take hold of them."* Now it made sense!

In spite of the tragedy, it was a happy reunion in Munich. Alan drove out to the airport with Fred as navigator. Unaccustomed to driving on the right hand side of the road, they almost drove down two expressways the wrong way. I was thankful they were there waiting when we disembarked. I recalled our sad parting in Sydney. How good it was to experience a reunion instead!

It took us the next few days to share all that God had been doing in our lives. We laughed and cried. We rejoiced in God's faithfulness. It had been rough going for both of us, but seeing God's hand in it made it all worthwhile. We discovered that the same day Alan had heard the message on "Giving up your Rights," I had heard almost the same message at Lugar Brae. We agreed that it was one of the hardest lessons to learn.

God had also been speaking to both of us about the future of our ministry, building the house of the Lord. Alan told me how he had felt led to visit the church in a nearby village, only to find the doors locked. The church was closed for repairs. He felt God was saying, "You are to help rebuild the house of the Lord." He also did a study on the book of Haggai, and felt God's reassurance that this was the vision He had for him.

Alan was allowed a more relaxed schedule now that his family was with him. He also had relief from his confined sleeping quarters. We had the luxury of our own tent, much to the girl's delight. We spread out corrugated cardboard on the damp ground under our air mattresses and sleeping bags. The children drew chalk streets all over the cardboard and amused themselves playing cars while Alan and I were in meetings.

Our days at the castle were full. Beth and Joy helped out in the print shop, where an enormous quantity of tracts and literature had to be sorted out. A treat for them was an occasional visit to the little village store to buy Mars bars. The storekeeper spoke German and we spoke English, but Mars bars, a delicious, chocolate-covered, caramel candy, were the same in both languages.

It was exciting for the family to spend every second day in Munich with the outreach teams. The day began with breakfast, which was quite a challenge! There were 900 people at the castle, and everything was prepared in huge quantities. Breakfast consisted of one hard-boiled egg and a thick slice of German bread. Its coarse, heavy texture was made more palatable with butter and plum jam. We lined up with our tinfoil plates to receive our portion.

Each person was given a bag lunch to eat in Munich: two slices of bread filled with German sausage, one large green apple and four plain cookies. All this went into one plastic bag, and, by lunchtime, the cookies had disintegrated into crumbs that coated the apple and the squashed sandwich. I had difficulty persuading the children that even if it didn't look appetizing, it would satisfy the hunger pangs. Dinner was back at the castle, usually a hot dish served on our tinfoil plates.

Munich was a quaint and beautiful city, with its paved walking streets, public gardens and old buildings. Every ledge or windowsill was an opportunity to display the glory of geraniums as they spilled out of their planters and hung in brilliant profusion.

At the Olympic Park we watched the athletes training for different events. It was fascinating to hear multitudes of people speaking so many languages. The groups in national costume, playing and performing dances, were a colorful sight. Even though we couldn't get into any of the Olympic events, we felt the excitement of this great international occasion.

We were excited to participate in YWAM's second march. The authorities had stopped the first march, but now, after the murder of the Israeli athletes, the German authorities allowed YWAM to march in the city. One police officer declared, "You are the only good thing that has happened in the last three weeks." They offered to cut ten thousand flowers from their city gardens for us to hand out as tokens of love and peace. Thousands of Christians marched in silence through the streets of Munich, handing out flowers and tracts and greetings of Jesus' love. People were openly moved. The horror of the murders had spread a blanket of sorrow over the city and made people much more open to the gospel. Hard hearts were softened. The march ended in front of the Town Hall in the center of Munich, and an immense crowd filled the Marienplatz to hear the good news of Jesus.

Our time in Munich was drawing to a close. The next part of our journey had yet to be determined. We believed God would make a way for us to go to England. We didn't know how. The girls and I had tickets on a KLM flight from Rotterdam to Sydney. Alan was booked on BOAC leaving London. He had assumed I would bring extra money when I joined him in Munich. I assumed the Lord would give Alan extra money. But, on the contrary, now neither of us had any money to pay our way from Munich to London. Alan had felt led to put every last cent he had into an offering days before I arrived.

What an interesting situation! In a strange land, far from home, with no money for food or transport. Of course, the Lord knew of our predicament, and even before we called on Him, He had the answer ready. We gathered with the others from Lugar Brae and prayed. Richard, the estate agent, came to us later. "I know you haven't any money," he told us. "I want you to have some of mine. I was given more than I needed back in Australia. I thought the Lord had a purpose in it. I believe the extra is for you."

The Olympic Games were now over. Some young people were staying on with YWAM. The majority made a mass exodus in cars, trains, and buses, heading for home or more travel. We left by bus, an 18-hour trip across Germany, up through Holland to Rotterdam, where we boarded a ferry to take us across the English Channel.

It was very late and we were weary. The boat was crowded and the best seats were already taken. We would have to try to sleep on the hard wooden benches. But before we even sat down or settled our things, a stewardess appeared and asked us to follow her. She ushered us to four thickly padded reclining seats in the first class section and said with a smile, "I think you will be more comfortable here."

God is so good! No sooner were we seated than the couple in front of us turned and offered two Mars bars. "The children might like them," they said.

Food and comfort—God's provision. We were grateful once more for God's tender care. We all felt a deep glow inside as the cabin lights were dimmed and everyone settled in for the night.

It was early morning when we sighted the English coast. We disembarked, caught a train to Liverpool Station in London, and took a taxi to Australia House. We camped ourselves and our luggage on the footpath outside. The busy metropolis of London swirled around us—buses, cars, and people all in a hurry to get somewhere. We knew where we wanted to go, but we were not sure how to get there. One small challenge we faced was we didn't have much money.

The three Australians who had joined our family for the trip in Britain, Richard Wills, Fred from our household, and Derek Brown from Faith Centre in Sydney, didn't have much either. So, we decided on the cheapest transport and accommodation possible—a camper van. A van would let us make our own schedule, cook our own meals and sleep on the road.

During the next two weeks, we had quite an adventure as seven of us crammed into a camper van designed to sleep four. Leaving London, we drove through England to Llanfairfechan, Wales where we visited my aunt Jean and cousin Dorothy. A memorable time for me was to go to Rhyl, the seaside town where I had spent the first eleven years of my life.

The house where I had been born, 51 Elm Grove, hadn't changed, though the field behind it where I had experienced God's presence was now built up with houses. I reflected on God's sovereign hand on my life, and I realized so much had happened in my life since that significant moment. Instead of continuing to live here in Wales, He had led my parents to Australia where I had met and married my husband, Alan, and now I had two precious daughters of my own.

Nothing had changed in Uncle John's house in Carlisle, Scotland. It was just as I remembered it. He had stocked his tiny kitchen with enough food to feed an army. We spent many hours talking, praying and sharing scriptures with him. There was a poem entitled *Then I Shall Know* on the bedroom dressing table.

> *Not 'til the loom is silent*
>
> *And the shuttles cease to fly,*
>
> *Will God unroll the canvas*
>
> *And explain the reason why.*
>
> *The dark threads are as needful*
>
> *In the weaver's skillful hands,*
>
> *As the threads of gold and silver*
>
> *In the pattern He has planned.*

Yes, God had woven the dark threads into our lives with the gold, causing all things to work together for our good and for His purpose. Uncle John himself had been a thread of gold woven through my life, and I was grateful to God for the chance to see him again. He was tearful as we said goodbye the next day.

It was Friday, September 22, and it was time to head back to London. Richard was due to fly out from Heathrow that afternoon. While he was waiting to board, we went to the KLM desk to inquire about our own seats. It was the end of the summer season, they told us, and flights were booked out. A staff concession ticket had no chance of a firm booking, even if it was accompanied by three regular fares, which the others had. Alan, Beth and Joy could leave, but I would have to wait indefinitely, maybe a month or more. It came as a bit of a shock. I thought my ticket problems were over when I left Australia.

Richard, meanwhile, had succeeded in getting his flight. We noticed a chapel across the road, the Chapel of St. George. I spent some time there alone with the Lord. Would I have to live through the delay experience again? I pictured Alan having to return to Australia, leaving me stranded in London. I recalled a dream Beth had had back in Australia, about being unable to leave a strange country. That was now a reality.

It was reassuring to think that God had prepared me for this, except for one thing—how long would the delay be? Alan assured me that we would all get back to Australia and he had no intention of leaving me behind. As we left the chapel the first person we saw was a KLM officer. We decided to go straight to the KLM office in the city. The office gave us no hope for a seat in the near future, so we asked for a refund on our tickets. We intended to go to Pan Am (parents of Qantas staff had concessions on Pan Am); perhaps they would make an exception for a sister.

The KLM clerk wrote out our refund and we took the credit voucher straight to Pan Am. We found the appropriate place at the long counter and explained our predicament to the Pan Am clerk. He looked at our voucher, made a few calculations and said reassuringly, "You have nothing to worry about. You have more than enough for two full fares and two half fares. You don't need to worry about a staff discount." Alan and I stared at him incredulously, then at each other.

"Look," he said, turning the paper around and pointing to the figures with his pen. "This is the cost of fares for the family from London to Sydney. The amount on the credit voucher is quite sufficient."

We stared at the figures. He was right. We could only conclude that a Pan Am fare was very cheap. We reserved four seats for the following Tuesday, September 26. I had to clear my ticket from Qantas, but it was now late and their office was closed. We would have to wait until the morning.

We should have felt relieved, but we had a nagging feeling that something wasn't right. We studied the figures given to us by the Pan Am ticket officer. How could one full fare, two half fares, and one concession fare on KLM pay for two full fares and two half fares on Pan Am with some left over? We made our own calculations. It dawned on us that the clerk at KLM had made a big mistake. She had refunded two full fares for the girls instead of two half fares. No wonder the Pan Am officer wasn't perturbed.

Well! What would we do now? We would return the credit voucher to KLM (we were sure God didn't want us to leave the country by dishonest means) and then we would be back in our impossible situation.

We were among the first customers at KLM the next morning. The same girl was embarrassed and grateful when we showed her the mistake. It could have cost her job, she said. Fortunately for her, the previous afternoon's business had not yet been processed. Apologizing profusely, she made out another credit voucher for the correct amount.

Now we had four seats reserved on Pan Am, but not the money to pay for them. God had to work something for us. With that conviction, we went to the Qantas office. The first person we spoke to said we could easily transfer my staff concession from KLM to Pan Am. Our relief was temporary. When the lady in charge checked it, she called us into her office. I was a sister, not a wife of Qantas staff, and so she informed us briskly, "There is no way you can transfer to Pan Am. It's against company rules." Seeing our dismay, she added, "Look, I'd like to help you, but I can't. You'll just have to wait until there's a seat available on KLM."

The four of us sat in a row facing her desk, waiting for something else to happen. Her face was a little flushed and she was obviously uncomfortable.

"Alright," she said after a long pause, "just sign these forms and I'll give you the transfer to Pan Am."

We asked what they were.

"Oh, they vouch that Mr. Langstaff works for Qantas."

"We can't sign them," we told her. "It wouldn't be right."

The woman flushed bright red. She looked ready to explode with frustration. "Well, what do you want me to do then?" she blurted through tense lips.

"Is there any chance of asking Pan Am to make an exception?" Alan asked.

I recalled a scripture God had given me during the delay back in Australia. It was a promise of receiving favor with those in authority. We need that favor now, Lord!

"I could call the personnel officer at Pan Am," she replied, "but they'd never agree to it."

"Would you be willing to try," Alan said apologetically, aware of her awkward situation, "and tell them the truth of our situation?"

"You want me to tell them everything?" she asked.

We nodded.

"All right, but they'll never agree to it."

She picked up the receiver, dialed Pan Am, and explained the predicament of the Australian family sitting in her office. Could they help? We watched her face intently. She said in a surprised tone, "You can help? Very well, I'll make the necessary changes."

She looked at us, her face relaxing in a half smile. "Pan Am is willing to help, much to my surprise, I admit. You can pick up your tickets on Monday and leave on the first available flight."

Praise the Lord! He had done it.

We spent the weekend with friends in Cambridge and it was with grateful hearts that we attended the Harvest Festival celebration in the village church. On Monday, we returned to London to pick up our tickets, booked for the next day. Alan and Derek returned the van. Dear Uncle John came all the way from Carlisle on the overnight train to see us off, bringing cakes and sweets for the journey, as well as £5.

We said our last goodbyes and boarded the plane for home. We had an interesting story to tell my brother David when he asked on our return, "How did you manage to fly home on Pan Am when only parents are allowed that concession?"

THE VISION UNFOLDS

CHAPTER 16

Go Build My House

"'Go up to the mountain, and bring wood, and build the house; and I will take pleasure in it, and I will be glorified,' saith the Lord."
Haggai 1:8 (KJV)

Alan had gone to America in 1971 with the vision of a Teen Challenge-type ministry in the Eastern Suburbs of Sydney. He came home with a different one—that of a national Charismatic conference. That vision had been sparked by the conversation with Ray Muller, who was organizing such a conference in New Zealand, and took shape at the International Charismatic Conference at Guilford in 1971.

The Guilford Conference was immensely significant for more than one reason. It was the first Charismatic conference Alan had attended and his first exposure to the Charismatic Renewal worldwide. It brought him into contact with many international leaders, particularly Michael Harper of The Fountain Trust. His vision of renewal in the Body of Christ matched our own. The Fountain Trust was to be the model for our own ministry, and the Guilford Conference was an example of what could happen in Australia. Alan and Ray Muller agreed to work together on two Charismatic conferences, one in New Zealand and one in Australia. They arranged complimentary dates and invited the same speakers. The stage was set for January 1973.

Alan had to return to the leaders in Sydney who had sent him to America. We felt the heavy weight of responsibility, not just to God, but to the men and women who had given us their support. It was not going to be easy to tell them of the new direction that God was leading us. It would look as though we were irresponsible and that we had used them.

Alan called them together to share with them what God had revealed. Every member of the distinguished group turned up. Our living room was packed. Alan found a place to sit on the edge of the table, his feet dangling. Everyone waited in silence, full of excited anticipation.

With a serious face, Alan began to share in a faltering voice, "Things have not worked out the way that we all expected on this trip. I discovered that God has called me, not to a work of rehabilitation, but to a work of renewal; not to set up a Teen Challenge ministry, but to hold a national Charismatic conference instead and bring together the different members of the Body of Christ."

The prophecy from the earlier meeting was making sense now. "You will blow the trumpet and gather my people together and build the walls."

The news came as a shock to most of the leaders. Not surprisingly, the atmosphere became subdued and tense. Then the questions came. Alan had no other answer than to say that God had used the Teen Challenge idea to get him going, so He could show him along the way what His real purpose was. God had called him to a ministry to the whole Body of Christ, and though his visit to Teen Challenge had been valuable and he was willing to help someone else set up a Teen Challenge ministry, God did not want him to take full responsibility for it.

It took some time for the leaders to understand what had happened. For some, understanding would not come until they saw the fruit of Alan's ministry many years later. It was a difficult decision for Alan to make, but he had no choice if he was to be obedient to the Lord.

Not all the leaders in the Sydney area shared Alan's enthusiasm. They weren't 100-percent convinced that Alan could direct a national Charismatic conference and one couldn't blame them for their doubts. After all, Alan had only been baptized in the Holy Spirit a short time and was an unknown newcomer as far as many were concerned. It must have looked like we were taking on too much, too soon. His experience in managing national conferences, which was rather different from organizing a local rally or seminar, was non-existent.

The same leaders expressed their doubts over the registration fee. We had no idea what to charge. Alan and I individually received direction from the Lord to charge ten dollars. It seemed a lot of money at the time, and evoked a good deal of criticism. We went ahead with the advertising, however, sure of God's guidance. Alan acted with a holy boldness and the faith to believe that, in God's strength, he could do it. After Alan got back from Munich, he knew he would need some help; he couldn't do it all on his own. So he shared the idea with Howard Carter of Logos Foundation. Howard agreed to cosponsor the conference and to provide some of the organizational backing.

That left us with a question mark. We needed a name for our ministry. We couldn't very well sponsor a Charismatic conference in the name of the Methodist Church. They might not appreciate it. Alan was fond of taking a walk around the block to think over such things. On such a walk, inspiration hit as he was passing the church. He returned, saying excitedly, "I've got it! We'll call it The Temple Trust."

The "Trust" part was inspired by The Fountain Trust in England, which served as our ministry model. The idea of the "Temple" came from a message by Bob Mumford, entitled "God's Divine Resistance."

Bob Mumford began the message with a prayer, "Oh, Lord Jesus, teach us Thy ways, show us Thy paths, change our understanding, redirect our thinking. Do what seemeth good unto Thee, oh Lord." He went on to give an analogy based on the book of Haggai. The exiles had returned to Jerusalem, but they were busy building their own houses, while the temple, God's house, lay in ruins. In the same way today, the Body of Christ was being neglected while Christians put their own houses in order. The Lord was seeking those who would build His temple, build His house, rather than their own.

It was not the first time that God had spoken to us from the book of Haggai. Some months before He had given us the same scripture, but while the vision was right, our application and interpretation of it was very wrong.

Alan and I owned a holiday cottage on the coast north of Sydney. Its main charm was not so much the big old house itself, which was rather dilapidated, but its glorious position overlooking MacMasters Beach. With a lot of hard work, it would have made an ideal retreat center for one or two families, or a small church group. All it needed were alterations and the money to carry them out. Not that we considered money a problem. After the trip to America, we knew that if God wanted us to do something, He would provide the means to do it.

In the meantime, it was a good place for relaxing and meditating as well as working hard. Alan and I went there to seek the Lord, and on one particular day I was sitting on the edge of the bed doing just that. From where I sat, I could look right down to the beach nestled in the shelter of the rocky cliff and hear the waves breaking on the shore below.

I picked up my Bible off the bedside table, opened it at random and began to read, *"'Go up to the mountains and bring wood and build the house, that I may take pleasure in it and be glorified,' saith the Lord,"* (Haggai 1:8). Quickly, I scanned the following verses. Could this be a word from the Lord?

His presence was so real. I read on, *"'The glory of this latter house shall be greater than the former,' saith the Lord. 'And in this place I will give peace,'"* (Haggai 2:9 KJV).

Excited, I shared it with Alan. What could it mean? We prayed and concluded that it applied to our holiday house, Orana Lodge. God must want us to remodel it as a retreat center. It would be a project to His glory. And of course, we could go ahead in faith that He would supply all we needed.

Our thoughts turned to practical matters. Plans had to be drawn. Alan had been an architect, but he had little time to spend on drawing. We were sure God wanted a thorough job done. So why not ask Noel Bell, who was both a friend and a fine architect?

We commissioned Noel to draw the plans and agreed to pay him a certain percentage after they were completed. He went to work at once and, on paper, the old house underwent a drastic transformation. Walls were to be knocked down, others were to be built, new rooms were to be added. The new Orana

Lodge would include a master bedroom suite and private balcony, a huge living room opening onto a deck, bunkrooms, and even a self-contained flat for the future caretaker. It was becoming what we dreamed it to be.

The finished plans were delivered. We had preliminary approval for a loan to cover both the building and the cost of the plans. Then we faced a crisis. The oil embargo in 1973 brought on a credit crunch and our application for the loan fell through at the last moment. It was a disaster. We had to take out a bank loan just to pay for the plans that had been drawn up. We were puzzled. Where had we gone wrong? We had had a clear word from God and had received it in faith. We had acted in obedience.

So why hadn't it worked out? We went back to Haggai, looking for our mistake. We were still sure the guidance was right. *"Go up to the mountain and bring wood and build the house..."* Perhaps we had taken it too literally, assuming that God meant us to take literal wood and build a literal house. Perhaps the interpretation was spiritual, not physical.

Gradually we began to understand. The house God was speaking about was the church—the Body of Christ. And the timbers, why, they were people, of course, to be brought together and built into a holy temple, a temple of living stones. God had finally been able to reveal the call He had for Alan and me: "Build My House!" In a time when so many were building their own houses, God wanted someone to build the larger house of the whole church.

For so long we had known of another calling beyond our own church. Yet, we had not connected the word with that call until God spelled it out in black and white. Now, it all came together—Haggai, the tape by Bob Mumford, and the national Charismatic conference. The conference was the beginning of a ministry that would gather together people from the whole Body of Christ and build the house of the Lord. So, The Temple Trust was born.

Australia's first National Charismatic Conference was held in January 1973, at the University of New South Wales. It gathered hundreds of people of all denominations from all over Australia. The evening meetings drew up to a thousand. The experienced ministry of Michael Harper, Kevin Ranaghan, Robert Frost and Winkie Pratney more than made up for Alan's inexperience. It was a small beginning, but God was doing something brand new.

The conference made an impact by its very existence, by the anointing of God upon it, and the spontaneity of life and joy in the Lord that flowed from it. It drew people together in a way that was good and pleasing to God. It opened their eyes to see what had been missing—brothers and sisters of faith coming together in harmony and unity.

Robert Frost from California gave a simple but striking illustration of what was happening as God poured out His Holy Spirit on the Body of Christ. On a large whiteboard he drew a number of small farmhouses, each with its own duck pond. Then he carefully drew barbed wire fences between each farm. These fences prevented the ducks on each farm from interacting with the others. Each set of ducks was happy with its own pond. Then Robert Frost drew large clouds in the sky. Rain poured down onto the farms. The water rose so high that the barbed-wire fences were covered, and the ducks discovered that they could swim back and forth over the fences that had divided them for so long. The ducks, he explained, were like Christians confined in their own denominations, and the heavy rainfall represented the widespread outpouring of the Holy Spirit.

Churches and pastors were blessed. Families were healed and restored. Individuals were touched by God. Those who came out of curiosity were more than satisfied. Those who were skeptical, including many pastors, began to see the great worth of what was happening. Even if they had reservations about Alan's youth and inexperience, they had to admit that God was doing something new and exciting.

The end of the Sydney conference really wasn't the end at all. It was just the beginning. It completed only a small part of what God had in mind for us to do.

CHAPTER 17

A Pathway of Faith

"By faith Abraham obeyed
when he was called to go out . . ."
Hebrews 11:8

"We have to leave Lugar Brae Church. I have just been told we are being replaced by another minister at the end of this year."

These were Alan's sober words as he returned home from a meeting with his superintendent minister and elders of the parish.

"What did you say?" I asked incredulously.

He repeated the words, "We have to leave Lugar Brae."

It was January 1973, just before the Sydney Conference. There was so much God wanted to do. How could this be happening now?

We were shocked at this news, even though we knew there were differences of opinion about the Charismatic Renewal and the Baptism of the Holy Spirit. Alan had been open and honest with the congregation, but most of them never entered into the new things that God was doing. Some of them were sympathetic, but only a handful were involved in the renewal.

The majority of the congregation didn't understand what we were doing. The trip to Munich had aroused great consternation. Alan had gone away while his superintendent was on long-service leave - not the wisest thing to do even if he did have permission. He had been called before the president of the Methodist Church after the Munich trip. He had not been charged with any misdemeanor because he had never broken any church law, even though he might have stretched it at times. The leadership was also concerned by Alan's growing involvement in the Charismatic Renewal.

The local congregation shared this concern. They represented an older generation who found it hard to accept change. They wanted things to stay as they had been for the past 10, 20, or 50 years. Even something simple like changing the time of the Christmas Day service from 7:30 a.m. to 8 a.m. aroused great opposition just because it had always been at 7:30 a.m. as long as anyone could remember.

After Alan was baptized in the Spirit, we had begun meetings in the parsonage every Monday night. These meetings made a significant contribution to the lives of many people. Alan was inexperienced in leading a Charismatic service, but he learned by doing.

Several of the local Spirit-filled pastors and leaders from the Eastern Suburbs met regularly for prayer and fellowship in our home. Toward the end of 1971, we had begun a series of Charismatic rallies once a month on Monday nights, with Dean Sherman as our first speaker.

The church was packed out. People had to sit in the choir stalls, down the aisles, even on the steps to the pulpit. They came from all over Sydney and in busloads from the southern suburbs. God poured out His Spirit, healed and delivered. There was tremendous life and spontaneity, scripture sung to music, praise and worship, a freshness, and a sense that God was doing something significant. It represented the early stage in Australia when God came down in glory and poured out His Spirit. It was exciting to be riding a new wave, carried by its ever-increasing power and strength.

The local congregation, however, did not share this excitement. They were apprehensive. The elders were seriously concerned that we would go through the floor. Apparently, there were white ants in the floorboards. The timbers didn't collapse until years later, but after some eight months, we were asked not to hold any more rallies.

In addition to the rallies, a small bookstore called The Upper Room was opened. It didn't make much money, but it was an effort to reach out with the written word for those who wanted to study and learn more about God's Word and ways. Alan began a School of the Bible and a fellowship meal on Wednesday evening.

In December 1972, Alan also organized a coffee shop called The Lost Coin. He got chicken pox in the middle of the six-week outreach, but the program went on without him. A team of young people spent their evenings out on the streets of Bondi Junction inviting people to come. By the end of the six weeks, crowds of teenagers were waiting at the door for it to open. Many of them were saved during the outreach. The Lost Coin was so successful that we wanted to make it permanent. To our dismay, the superintendent minister and the elders said no.

Not only did we minister to young people outside the church, but we also had a number staying with us in the parsonage, varying from one to nine, from short-term boarders such as Jim, a drug addict who had been with us for nearly three months, to people like Carna, who was studying to be a kindergarten teacher and lived with us for three years.

The people in the church didn't show any desire to have extended households, but didn't make any objections about ours. The young people brought life and support into the church.

By now there were quite a number of people who were committed to renewal, all on fire and ready to go. We could have easily started our own church, but we never considered doing such a thing. All our focus, planning, and attention locally had included Lugar Brae. We had many dreams for Lugar Brae, and there was much more that we felt God wanted us to do. We felt we had only just begun.

We dreamed of creating a renewal and teaching center on the properties next to the church. We walked past these houses almost daily, claiming them for the Lord. We knew every detail of their appearance. We spent many hours individually and together praying and seeking God's will. On one occasion, Ray, Alan and I were praying in the church when the Lord gave us a scripture from Ezekiel about measuring the temple. We took God's Word literally and thought it applied there and then. Alan began to pace out the length and breadth of the church. If we included the adjacent properties, we could erect a good-sized building with an underground parking lot—the renewal center we were sure God wanted. We should have learned our lesson from the house at MacMasters, but we thought this time it was different. We were wrong again.

Actually, God was speaking about the dimensions of His spiritual temple, a living temple not made by human hands. Its dimensions spread across the whole world, embracing people of all nations, races, and colors, going far back into history and stretching forward to include those not yet born into His Kingdom.

An important part of our dream had been to acquire a bigger house. The parsonage was jammed with people and was in constant use for meetings, bible studies, counseling and visitors. We had prayed increasingly for a house where we would have more room for our household and our ministry. On one of our many walks around the block, we had noticed a lovely old house, set back from the road and bordered by a stone wall. It was not for sale, and it would have been well out of our price range had it been, but we began to pray about it. Maybe the Lord wanted us to have it. Its location was ideal. It had a back entrance onto a lane that led to Lugar Brae Church.

We met the owner on the very day she was moving out. We could hardly believe it. The foundations had been damaged when builders were excavating the lot next door to make way for high-rise apartments, she explained. She showed us the caved in ceiling and floor in the living room. Afraid that the whole house would fall in on her, she was moving out.

We told her that if she ever decided to sell, we would be interested in buying. Sometime later, she did decide to sell. Excited, we borrowed a key and went to look through the house. This was an ideal opportunity to claim the promise that everywhere we put the soles of our feet would be ours. It was certainly a gracious home. I had always wanted a house with old style charm and this house was full of it. It had a wide veranda with an ocean view and a red-carpeted staircase leading up to bedrooms that were equally charming with their sloped ceilings. It was big enough to accommodate our family and guests, and it had a large meeting room where we could hold Bible classes.

It felt like it was almost ours. We would call it Salem—our little bit of the Promised Land. We were sure that we would live there one day. We offered 50 thousand dollars for the house. We didn't have the money, but we were sure that the Lord would supply it if He wanted us to have it. We persevered in faith and prayer and kept in regular contact with the owner. It was a valuable house in a nice area and she was looking for offers starting at 100 thousand dollars. Eventually, after a long time, she sold it to someone else for 75 thousand dollars.

We were puzzled and disappointed. It seemed that God had spoken to us about the house. Perhaps we had made a mistake. We gained some insight about properties from Ralph Wilkerson when he came to Australia for the next conference in Canberra. "God," he said, "will often get your sights on something, not because He wants to give it to you, but because He wants to motivate you to begin to believe and seek Him."

There is a verse in the Bible that says, *"'For My thoughts are not your thoughts, nor are your ways My ways,' says the Lord," (Isaiah 55:8).* There was much wisdom in those words for novices like us, who were trying to explore and discover the mind of the Lord. They explained why things didn't always work out the way we thought they would. We just had to accept that as part of God's dealing in our lives. He was teaching us to trust Him. Proverbs 3:5-6 reads, *"Trust in the Lord with all your heart, and lean not on your own understanding. In all your ways acknowledge Him, and He shall direct your paths."*

And now we were being asked to leave Lugar Brae. There was so much we didn't understand. Why was God allowing us to be replaced at Lugar Brae? Just as things were really beginning to happen! Why were the people unable to accept the move of the Holy Spirit? God had promised to fill the church with His glory and in a certain measure He had done so. If only we could have more time, more cooperation from the leadership in the parish. We believed that God wanted to establish a city set on a hill that would draw people to it from far away, to be taught His truths and learn to walk in His ways.

Had all this been our imagination? Surely not. It seemed as though any sign of life and fruit from Alan's ministry in the Methodist church was being cut off.

Our initial reaction was to fight the decision. There were so many things to be accomplished at Lugar Brae and in the Eastern Suburbs area. We knew the Lord called us here, and unless the Lord called us out, we had to stay. But if we wanted to remain in the Methodist church, we would have to accept a pastorate elsewhere, perhaps in the country. The alternative was to leave the Methodist church altogether.

"God, what do You want us to do?"

The answer soon came to Alan as he was speeding along the freeway. He and Jim Glennon were taking Michael Harper to the airport after the Charismatic Conference. The conversation turned to Alan's future. Should he fight to keep his position at Lugar Brae church? What should he do?

Both men strongly challenged Alan, saying "God is using the decision by the church to replace you as a means of thrusting you out into a full-time renewal ministry."

Their words broke something in Alan and he immediately recognized that God's hand was in all that was happening.

Later, Alan was invited to Faith Center for a presbytery meeting, a small gathering of mature spiritual leaders who prayed and prophesied over people. There he received a significant prophecy that confirmed God's hand on our lives. The prophecy used the language of old-time Pentecostalism.

"There are many that watch thee, saith the Lord, and say in their hearts, 'What shall this man do?' Thou hast said even unto Me, 'Yea, what shall I do?'

"Behold, your path has been a plain path, but the Lord has brought thee to a junction, He has taken thee off the stream that thou hast known and would cause thee even to run a new course. He would say unto you this night, leave and forget the things that are behind you, for behold, I would teach you new things, yea and in a new way would I lead thee. Thou shalt not even remember the former things, for My ways shall be diverse, they shall be ways that shall be new to thee. I shall teach thee and lead thee in a way that thou hast not been heretofore, My hand shall be with thee, yea, I shall supply thy need.

"Thou shalt say, 'Lord, where is my supply?' And behold, when thou wilt seem to come to even the end of thyself and shalt come even to the end of the barrel of meal, and seem to have but a handful and the cruse of oil shall seem to be dry, yet shall I cause it even to come again and again, and thou shalt find that which thou dost need shalt be sufficient for that hour and for that time. And I shall lead you in a new path—it shall be a pathway of faith, for thou hast asked Me to lead thee this way. Thou shalt learn new principles and new ways of faith shall I teach thee. Thou shalt know enlargement, for not only do many watch thee at this time, but as thou art successful in Me, many, yea, shall be encouraged even to follow thee. Thou shalt be one that shall speak unto them and say, 'The Lord has been faithful unto me. Yea, if thou dost go, the Lord shall be faithful unto thee as He hath been unto me.'

"I do send thee even as a spearhead, even as a pioneer, yea even as a fine leader, even as a trailblazer will I make thee and many shall follow thee because of the faith that I shall instill within thy heart. Yea, not only in thine heart shall it be, saith the Lord, but thou shalt impart that faith to others. For I place a word of faith in thine heart that is not of thyself at this time, but I shall work it within thine life. Thou shalt speak with assurance and authority and conviction. Thou shalt know the goodness of thy God that doth lead thee."

We began to understand what God was doing. He was forcing Alan out of the parish into a wider ministry to the whole Body of Christ, a ministry he couldn't carry out if he stayed in the local church. So, in the end, we didn't fight the decision. We agreed to leave peacefully and to move out in faith, believing that the Lord had it all under His control. In fact, we left six months earlier than we had to.

The new minister was coming back from America in the middle of 1973, and we felt we should let him take over the church and move into the parsonage. This meant we had to find another place to live. Our dreams of living in the big house had never been fulfilled. At that time, it was still empty, but God had not opened the door for us. Sadly, we laid down that dream at the feet of Jesus.

We felt that the Lord wanted us to stay on that particular block, so we began walking around it, believing God for a house. As the date for moving drew uncomfortably close, we decided to walk around the block, declaring, "Lord, let there be a house on this block for us today."

On the way home, we paid a visit to our real estate agent, Richard Wills, to see if there was a house available. It was not our first such visit. This time, we told him we believed God was going to provide a house for us that day. And sure enough, there was a house available.

"We've just had a phone call from the owners of a house—Number 30 MacPherson Street," he said.

It was the right block!

"The tenants have disappeared without paying the rent. The house is due to be demolished in a few months, but you can rent it in the meantime."

He took us across the road to see it. It wasn't the mansion we were believing for—it was the farthest thing from it! It was obvious why they planned to demolish it, as it was the worst house on the entire block. To call it dilapidated was an understatement! But God had told us He would provide a house that day, and this was the only one available. So we had to accept it. God seemed to blind our eyes to just how terrible it was. And, praise God, by that time I was ready to accept anything. We were excited, as we knew we were moving into a whole new realm of faith.

Carna, the girl who was staying with us, wasn't quite so excited. She walked in the front door of her new home, took one appalled look and kept walking straight out the back door.

We had offered to move out of the parsonage in July so that the new minister and his family could move in. Michael Harper had invited Alan to the Fountain Trust Conference in Nottingham in early July, so we had to start moving in June. Alan shifted all the furniture into Number 30 before he left and arranged for a young man to help move our belongings while he was in Nottingham. The young man didn't show up, however. I had no money to hire someone, so I had to take on the mammoth task myself. Fortunately, our new house was only fifty yards from the back gate of the parsonage, so we didn't have far to move. I loaded our belongings—pots, pans, dishes, and Alan's books—into an old baby pram and pushed it down the lane to Number 30. By the time all the things were moved, I was exhausted and had developed tennis elbow with all the lifting, pulling, and pushing.

Our two cats, Buffy and Fluffy, bewildered by all the activity, spent several days trailing the pram back and forth. Neither they nor our collie, Lassie, could work out which house we were living in. The cats finally found the two comfortable old chairs that Alan had bought at the church opportunity shop for two dollars each and made Number 30 their home.

The parsonage furniture, of course, had to remain. We had a refrigerator to take with us, as we had been given an extra one some time earlier, and it seemed a luxury at the time. It turned out to be the Lord's provision in advance.

Alan and I had no bed to take with us. We had bought a new innerspring mattress on moving to the parsonage, but after donating it to the parsonage we could hardly take it with us. We were left with the original mattress that was folded up in the garage. It had no springs left and it was in as bad a shape as Number 30. The only bed we had was a three-quarter size (which was too small for the mattress) that had been left behind in the house. So, we cut off a few inches from an old-fashioned panel door and nailed that across that base.

To make things even more interesting, we didn't have a bedroom at Number 30 in which to put our makeshift bed. The house had only two bedrooms. Our daughters, Beth and Joy, had one and we gave Carna the other, which was not much of a gift. As a boarder, we felt she should have a room. She was studying at kindergarten training college and had a great deal of work to do. So we made the living room into a makeshift bedroom and hung a sheet across it to give us a little privacy. Back in the parsonage when we had people stacked up in double bunks and sleeping in the garage, I could retreat to my bedroom and think, *Well, I'm married, so I'll never have to give up my bedroom. The Lord can't ask me to give it up because we have to be in a room by ourselves.* Little did I know then that God would ask me to give up my right to a bedroom.

By the time we moved all our belongings and cleaned the parsonage, it was almost time for the new minister to arrive. Carna was the last one to leave. She was having her last decent shower in the parsonage bathroom just before they arrived. She went out the back door almost as the new occupants were arriving at the front door.

After seeing the bathroom at Number 30, one could understand why she was having one last shower. It was in a bad way. The bath was too stained and dirty to clean. We couldn't have a bath in it, so we put down a mat on the bottom and stood on that to take a shower, trying not to touch the bath at all. The sink was clogged with thick layers of paint and dirt, and I had to use a chisel to get it clean.

As Alan and I were occupying the living room, we turned the small dining room into a living-dining room. I freshened it up by papering the end wall, and also painted the kitchen window and back door and garden seat outside with a dark brown glossy paint. White crossovers at the kitchen window added a finishing touch. Now it looked more like home. We would only be there a short time, so we would manage. After all, we had a roof over our heads, a sunny back lawn and a park across the street. We were happy there in that humble house that the Lord provided.

The contrast between this humble house and the one we had been believing God for was so great that it was hard to believe they were on opposite ends of the same block. From our back door we could see the roof of the other house, a constant reminder that God sometimes leads us down a low road before taking us up to great things. We learned the principle of going down before the Lord takes you up. As the Bible says, *"Humble yourselves in the sight of the Lord, and He will lift you up," (James 4:10).*

This was living by faith. When you set out to do something new, you start at the very beginning, or the very bottom.

CHAPTER 18

Despise Not The Day
Of Small Beginnings

"Though your beginning was small,
yet your latter end would increase abundantly."
Job 8:7

We had a place to live, but now we needed an office. We considered using the small, enclosed veranda at Number 30, that is until it rained and we discovered that the roof leaked. The floor was so crooked that nothing would sit straight on it. The Lord obviously had something else in mind.

But where could we find an office? And if we did, how could we afford the rent? Richard Wills, the real estate agent, came to the rescue again. His firm owned a small shop across the road next door to their office, which we could rent for the ridiculous price of six dollars a month.

Our new office was a tiny rectangle with a corner cut out, measuring just twelve by seven feet. It was barely big enough to hold Alan's desk and a secondhand sofa that I covered with brown fabric. After we papered the walls and spent five dollars on a 20-year-old typewriter, we were ready to do business for the Lord.

Our little office was a pleasant place, with a large sunny window overlooking a park. We had no secretary, of course. Alan used two or three fingers to type his own letters and I used two or three fingers to type cassette tape labels.

When Michael Harper invited Alan to a conference in Nottingham, England that July, he had sent half the airfare and Alan cashed an insurance policy to pay the rest. He had a strange feeling about the trip, that he was "only just going to make it." He went to the airport to find that the copilot had been rushed to the hospital with food poisoning and the flight was delayed 12 hours. On the way back from Nottingham, in the airport at Delhi, he sensed the presence of evil and began to intercede and pray in tongues. A flock of birds flew into two engines during the critical period of takeoff and they both caught fire. The plane had to make an emergency landing at Bombay accompanied by blaring fire trucks down the runway. He only just made it.

Alan's budget did not include any extras, like accommodation, so when he arrived in London he spent the night stretched out on a couple of airport seats. He was startled awake by the pressure of a firm hand on his shoulder. A big London Bobbie was looking down at him. "Do you have an airline ticket? If not, you have to move out of the airport," he said. Alan quickly produced his ticket, relieved that he wasn't being arrested for loitering.

The Nottingham Conference gave him deeper insight into the Renewal and contact with leaders such as Graham Pulkingham and Larry Christenson. Michael Harper took up a thanksgiving offering for seven organizations, and nearly $1500 went to our ministry. This gave us the money to begin planning our next conference.

Earlier that year, we had been impressed that God wanted the conference to be held in a city other than Sydney. God had called us to the Eastern Suburbs, but that was only part of the vision. The vision extended to the whole Body of Christ in Australia.

We had already planned a month's vacation in May with two things in mind: to expand our horizons of Australia; and to find the city for the next National Charismatic Conference. If we were to have a national ministry, then we needed to get a feel for the country and the people. We sold our station wagon and bought a Toyota camper van. That camper van was our home for the next month, and it earned the name "Fruit of the Spirit Machine," since living in such confined quarters was very demanding.

The thousand-mile journey from Sydney to Adelaide seemed endless. The monotony was broken only by taking turns driving and seeing a stray kangaroo. Adelaide, the city of churches and parks, was dressed in sparkling autumn color. Alan left the children and me in a motel in Adelaide while he flew to Perth to speak at a conference. On his return, our journey took us along the majestic rugged cliffs of the South Coast of Victoria, then inland along winding mountain roads, the van slithering round rainsoaked curves. The little farmhouses nestled into grassy slopes above the lush green valleys were a refreshing change from the city bustle.

Melbourne, on the Yarra River, the center of business and commerce, brought us back to reality. In one of the huge parks, I felt like Maid Marian as I sat under the trees and put the finishing touches on a green velvet skirt and jacket to wear at the Full Gospel Businessmen's banquet that evening.

Throughout this journey, we were very much aware that we were turning our backs on the past and going where we had never been before. God provided a vivid illustration of this when on one of the country roads we crossed over a creek on a brand new bridge. Workmen were burning the old one. The huge rustic timbers were charred black as the flames found their way up through the cracks. We had often heard the saying about "burning your bridges behind you," but we were amazed to actually witness it. It was sad, too, to watch the old give way to the new, to watch the labor of long ago go up in smoke. We couldn't help but apply it to ourselves. God was leading us in new ways, and there was to be no turning back to the old ways.

We prayed in each city, somewhat like Nehemiah going out to observe the broken walls of Jerusalem. One day we felt that God's people would be gathered together in every major city of Australia. The walls would be repaired and the temple of the Lord restored.

The last city we visited was Canberra, the carefully-planned capital of Australia, beautiful with its man-made lake and tree-lined streets. Alan had a strong conviction that our next national conference should be there. While we had been praying about the conference back in Sydney, Beth had a dream where she saw a map of a city with a river running through it. All we had to do was identify the city in her dream. But none of the maps of the cities we had already visited matched her dream.

Now in Canberra, Alan visited the university and trusting he was doing the right thing, booked the auditorium and accommodation for the following January. He brought back some brochures and maps of the university to the van with him. Beth and Joy browsed through a couple of the spare copies, chattering. Then there was a stunned silence. I turned around. Beth's face was full of utter surprise.

"What's the matter?" I asked.

She looked down at the open map, which was an aerial view of the Canberra University. "This is it!" she said. "It is exactly as I saw it in my dream. There is even a river running through it."

What a wonderful confirmation that this was the place!

The Lord used Beth in many ways, giving her visions and words about things she had no knowledge of—an encouragement to us in our new spiritual walk.

We were satisfied that God had guided us on this trip, and given us insight and contacts with people who would prove invaluable as the ministry expanded.

The trip itself was not without trauma. One of Beth's cats, Fluffy, had taken seriously ill with feline anemia. Reluctantly, we had to leave her in the care of Warwick, the young man next door who was kind enough to come over and give her daily medication. Twice during the trip, God woke me to intercede for Fluffy to live. Warwick later told us that there were two occasions when he thought Fluffy was not going to make it. She was still very ill when we got back and had not responded to the medication. The vet did not expect her to live. She was so agitated that we decided to stop giving her the pills and trust God to heal her.

Fluffy disappeared to die—or so we thought. Although we were sad, we had a tremendous peace. The next morning I went into the laundry and there was Fluffy, obviously better. In a few days the healing was complete.

The cats and our collie, Lassie, were an important part of our family and God proved His faithfulness to us through them. A few months later, Buffy, Fluffy's twin, fractured a hind leg. The vet ordered three weeks' confinement to give the leg a chance to heal. In our house, that was a difficult task. That morning, a pastor friend, Allan Alcock, called to see

Alan. Buffy limped in painfully and settled in an old armchair. We asked Allan to pray for her healing. To our delight, Buffy jumped down from the chair and walked on all four feet, completely healed. God's healing love isn't confined to humans, it extends out to all His creation.

In September, it was time to move again. Number 30 was about to be demolished. So around the block we went again, praying, "Lord, let there be another house."

God answered our prayers. A house right across the road from the office was vacant and for rent. So we repeated the old procedure, loading chairs and boxes into the pram and pushing it fifty yards back and forth along the footpath between Number 30 and Number 42 McPherson Street. Number 42 was a big improvement on Number 30, although it only had two bedrooms. This time Alan and I would have to sleep in the dining room.

Our lives were certainly not boring. There was always something to challenge or test us. One day, however, exceeded anything we could have anticipated.

We were driving our daughter Joy to St. Catherine's Girls School on the first day of the new school year. As we were coming up the hill toward the school gate, we were flagged down by the mother of one of Joy's friends. Waving frantically, she cried out, "There is a man over there assaulting a woman!"

We were horrified to see that across the street in the entryway to a block of apartments, a man with his back toward us had his hands around the throat of a woman. At the same time, he was beginning to bash her head against the brick wall. She was holding a baby in her arms, unable to protect herself. Something had to be done to stop him before he murdered her.

We both quickly realized the man was bigger and stronger than Alan. I knew he had to help, but knew he would be in danger also if he did. I flashed a prayer to the Lord. "What can we do?"

Alan was opening the van door. The Lord's answer came back strong and clear. "Tell him to use the name of Jesus!"

Everything seemed to be in slow motion as I saw Alan step down from the van. "Use the name of Jesus!" I called out after him.

Alan ran across the road to the sidewalk, then raised his hand and shouted out, "In the name of Jesus, stop!"

Instantly it was as if the man was struck with a bolt of lightning from heaven. He let go of the woman's throat, staggered back five or six paces, fell over an iron balustrade and landed prostrate on the ground, motionless.

The police soon arrived and after interrogating the man, arrested him. He did not want to be taken away and it took all the strength of those two policemen to put him in what Australians call a "paddy wagon." Still clutching her baby, the woman was rushed off to receive medical help and we never saw her again.

We found out later that she was the man's wife. About a year earlier he had bought a Ouija board and had opened himself up to demonic influence. He was practicing what is called automatic writing, and was writing a new Bible. That morning an evil spirit told him, "You are to kill your wife because she has Jewish blood in her veins." After he was released from custody, we tried to help him. Other people tried as well, but he never could make a breakthrough and eventually committed suicide.

Besides saving the life of the woman, this experience taught us that there is amazing power and authority in the name of Jesus. Days like this made moving house and planning conferences seem rather ordinary.

It was October, and publicity for the Canberra Conference in January 1974 needed to go out, but Ralph Wilkerson from Melodyland Christian Center in California had not yet replied to our invitation to be the main speaker. We also wanted to announce it at a rally being held that night in a nearby Anglican church. This prompted Alan to call California from the office, but he couldn't reach him. We were sure that Ralph Wilkerson was the man for the Canberra Conference, so Alan knew he had to persevere until he got through. Finally, he came home to dinner, leaving a friend, Fred, who wanted to stay in the office and practice his guitar.

Ten minutes later, an excited, breathless Fred charged in the front door, trying to get the words out of his mouth. "Quick, It's David Wilkerson on the phone, calling from America! He wants to talk to you!"

He had the first name wrong. It was Ralph Wilkerson, but that small mistake didn't matter. Alan pushed his chair back from the table, ran out of the house and across the road to the office to snatch up the phone. "Pastor Wilkerson, it's Alan Langstaff here. I've been trying to reach you."

"Yes, I know," was the reply. "I'm calling because of that. I have decided to come to Australia in January." He explained that he had already sent a letter declining the invitation to speak at the conference and was surprised to hear that we hadn't received it. That morning, he had received the guidance that he was to reverse his decision and go to Australia.

Alan was excited to hear the news he had been waiting and believing for. "That's great," he said, "I really believe you are the man God wants here in Australia at this time."

God's timing was perfect. Ralph Wilkerson's refusal arrived in the mail the next morning. If Alan had read the letter, he would not have even tried to call. Now we could send out publicity for the conference. A young man by the name of Frank volunteered to help in the office, and on one occasion we hired a temporary secretary for the day to do a lot of the typing and correspondence. Registrations began to trickle in.

Two weeks before the conference, Alan sat down and did a rough check of the budget. He realized that the finances were a disaster. We were going to lose thousands of dollars and Alan and I were the only ones responsible. There was no board, no church and no sharing the load with Howard Carter as with the first conference. We alone were responsible to pay all the bills.

Alan went for a walk in the park across the street and cried out to the Lord. "Lord, what are you doing? You've called me to run a conference that looks like it's going to be a financial disaster!"

He felt the Lord speak to his heart and say, "If you can't handle failure, how can I trust you with success?"

So Alan continued the preparations and we went into the conference expecting to lose money, expecting that we would have to sell our beach house and our belongings to pay the debt. We determined that whatever happened, we were going to follow the call that the Lord had given us. To follow the Lord meant that we might lose everything.

We discovered that the Lord had already been ahead of us, anticipating our needs. As Ralph Wilkerson motivated people toward faith and the vision for Australia, he encouraged them to stand with us. On Thursday night, he asked if he could take up a special offering. He invited people to give whatever they could, even sacrificially, and come and put it on the stage, which served as an altar. A girl gave her most prized possession—a tape recorder. Another gave the proceeds of a thousand-dollar painting he had sold.

We also placed a gold box near the entrance. Two thousand dollars were placed in it. God was faithful! He moved on the hearts of the people to give. The conference didn't end in failure, but in success! Instead of debts, we had enough to move to a larger office and buy office furniture and a typewriter. The conference also produced a full-time secretary named Anne. She felt called to give up her job to work at half her previous salary for The Temple Trust. She was an answer to prayer.

Ralph and Alan had a number of talks together. When Ralph's plane was delayed leaving Canberra Airport, they took the opportunity to talk. He shared from his own experience and imparted to Alan a vision of the world and a faith in a God who could do great things. Alan, with few years and little experience behind him, was ready to learn all he could from men who were anointed leaders.

Murray Cameron, who led the worship at the conference, was one of the first Pentecostals to stand with Alan. He became a real brother in the Lord over many years. It was wonderful to see so many people being blessed, healed, or delivered, and baptized in the Spirit. Our travel agent, Harry Hollister, was one of them. There was also a strong prophetic anointing on that conference. Words were given about pioneers reaching into all areas of Australia and tiny fires being lit all across the nation, fires that would one day become a huge blaze.

The Canberra Conference was over, but the vision of bringing renewal, restoration, and revival to Australia had just exploded. That explosion would have quite an impression on the spiritual destiny of this vast continent.

Not only did Ralph Wilkerson prove to be God's man for the hour as far as the conference was concerned, but perhaps more importantly, he imparted to Alan, personally, a whole new vision—a dimension of faith—for what God was wanting to do through The Temple Trust.

CHAPTER 19

The Right Word At The Right Time

"Your ears shall hear a word behind you, saying,
'This is the way, walk in it.'"
Isaiah 30:21

The Temple Trust was beginning to grow, and we moved out of the one-room office and into 151 Clovelly Road. The new staff hardly knew what to do with themselves in what seemed an enormous two-story building. They were hard pressed to fill the ground floor!

The offering at the Canberra Conference made all of this possible. God had provided in abundance, including the partitioning, an air conditioning unit, carpet and furniture worth at least $4,000. "All I can give you is $1,500 for it," Alan had told the owner. He gulped, but after consulting with his partner, accepted.

Later that same year in August, the children and I joined a tour to the United States led by Allan Alcock and arranged by The Temple Trust, to attend the Charismatic Clinic at Melodyland Christian Center. Alan was also invited to be one of the speakers. It was during that Clinic that he had a significant meeting with Dick Mills, a minister from the United States who has a unique prophetic ministry with words of knowledge.

On the Wednesday night following the evening service, Alan felt restless. He had a distinct impression God was wanting to say something to him, but what was it? We prayed together in the hotel room, believing God would speak clearly as He had done so many times before. Alan prayed, "Lord if you want to say something to me, I want to hear it."

He wasn't prepared for the speedy and rather unusual way God answered that prayer.

Still restless, he went downstairs and at about 11 p.m. found himself standing in the hotel lobby, conscious he was there for some reason, but not really understanding why. Then the main door opened and in walked Vic Ramsey (an old acquaintance of Alan's from England) and with him a man Alan had seen on the platform but had never met in person before, Dick Mills.

No sooner had they been introduced than Dick looked Alan in the eye. "I have some scriptures from the Lord for you," he said, proceeding to quote a number of Bible verses. They all had to do with expansion and the widening ministry God was going to give to us. The most significant was from Isaiah 54:2-3: *"Enlarge the place of your tent, and let them stretch out the curtains of your dwellings; do not spare; lengthen your cords, and strengthen your stakes. For you shall expand to the right and to the left..."*

Standing in the lobby of the Grand Hotel following his sovereign encounter with Dick Mills, Alan was stunned. I listened in awe as he shared with me back in the hotel room. What did it mean God was going to expand our ministry? How would that happen? We would soon find out.

In contrast to 1974, which was largely a year of consolidation for The Temple Trust—a time of settling into new offices, the commencement of Vision Magazine and the tape lending library, and the organizing of the first American tour to Melodyland Christian Center—1975 proved to be a year of rapid expansion.

It began in January with the Melbourne conference, the biggest that The Temple Trust had ever held. Both financially and numerically it was a breakthrough. As crowds of over 2,500 squashed into Dallas Brooks Hall, they were exposed to a new dimension of praise and unity.

Financially, the conference could have been a disaster. During the year The Temple Trust had stepped out beyond its resources and was $12,000 in debt. But at a special offering taken up by Canon Jim Glennon on the Thursday night, people freely gave over $18,000, which rescued us.

The vision for having this conference in Melbourne had been birthed a whole year before when Alan and I were preparing for the conference in Canberra. It was just a week prior to that conference when Alan and I and a Temple Trust staff member, Frank Barbara, were in our living room when, in one of those sovereign twists of conversation, we found ourselves talking about the next year's conference and the fact that next time it should be in Melbourne.

As we were speaking, the Spirit of God fell upon Alan in a rather unusual way. Kneeling on the floor, he went through an experience of literally feeling like a worm before God. In the words of Isaiah 41:14, *"Fear not, you worm Jacob . . . I will help you,"* he needed to know that the Lord alone was his strength and that to Him alone went all the glory.

Sometime later, while we were looking for a suitable venue for the conference, God again sovereignly revealed His hand and set His seal on the conference. We were driving a hired car around Melbourne, looking at various places for accommodation. We had already eliminated quite a few as unsuitable, when we came across a beautifully tree-lined street. Without even knowing what buildings were on the street, instinctively we knew in our spirits that this was it. Only later did we discover how ideal the choice was. The street housed a number of large university colleges, as well as suitable auditoriums for the daytime sessions.

In continuing fulfillment of Dick Mills' prophecy, the conference ushered in a whole year of expansion for The Temple Trust. It began with the sponsoring of the Jim Spillman Crusade in March. His anointed ministry was followed up and complemented both by Fred Price, with his strong message on faith, and by Dick Mills, with his powerful prophetic ministry.

Jim Spillman's ministry was of particular importance. Jim, who for many years was, in his own words, "a bull-headed Baptist preacher," experienced a revolutionary turnabout in his ministry when he was baptized in the Spirit in 1972. Somewhat reminiscent of Kathryn Kuhlman, he entered into an outstanding ministry in the area of miracles.

When he arrived in Sydney, Jim was an unknown. He stepped straight off the plane to speak at a Holy Spirit teaching seminar. By the end of the week, up to 1,500 were coming to hear him. He was God's man for the hour. His ministry combined inspirational preaching, contagious humor, and a powerful demonstration of the Holy Spirit. Some people involved in the Charismatic Renewal were somewhat skeptical of the experience of being "slain in the Spirit." Jim was able to demonstrate the power of God in a refreshing, dynamic way that Australians could more readily accept. To quote a young teenager who was converted at his meetings, "I never realized Christianity could be fun!"

I was personally impacted by Jim Spillman's ministry. At a church in our area, I responded to his altar call.

"Come here, dear," he said, beckoning me with his finger. "That's very interesting. Has the Lord been talking to you about writing a book?" he asked.

I commented that if God did, I would call it The Agony of Obedience. Everyone in the church laughed at that point.

He continued on in a serious tone. "My instructions for you are, begin to write immediately. It is needed yesterday. Yesterday it is needed!"

Me write a book? I thought, rather skeptical of the idea. God would have to convince me that it was His will. He eventually did and you are reading that book now.

THE MINISTRY GROWS

CHAPTER 20

That They May Be One

"That they all may be one, as You, Father, are in Me, and I in You; That they also may be one in Us, that the world may believe that you sent Me."
John 17:21

Around the block we went again, praying, "Let there be a house." In the midst of this busy time of ministry, we found it necessary to move again. Our present house, too, was to be demolished to make room for more shops. What would God provided this time?

Sure enough, there was a two-story house for rent on the north side of the block. It had been an elegant house once upon a time and had a lot of potential for anyone with money. We took the upstairs apartment and Ray, his wife Jane, and Frank took the downstairs. We had our own bedroom at last. It was a huge room with two French doors opening onto an old veranda. We made a few improvements with paint and wallpaper, all that our finances would allow.

The house did have its drawbacks. Not one window had any view whatsoever. We were hemmed in on both sides by the sight of concrete walls and rooftops. Both the veranda and the back stairs were supported by rotten timber and had to be used in faith. The antiquated gas stove was emitting more gas through the rusty pipes than through the jets. It was threatening to blow up any minute and we needed to replace it. We made Number 329 home, however. The girls loved all its odd nooks and crannies. We were only a few yards from their school.

Now maybe I could take some time to recover from the pressured demands of conferences and moving. Nevertheless, there was no speedy recovery. Instead, I seemed to grow more weary.

It took every ounce of strength to climb the long stairs of the old house at 329 Bronte Road. My back was hurting and I was so weak that I began to think that something was physically wrong with me. No doubt the stress of the past years, including all the moves from one house to another, had taken its toll. I felt like an old lady ready for retirement.

A visit to the doctor did little to reassure me. Tests revealed nothing. The problem was stress and tension, announced the doctor, and he prescribed tranquilizers. I took them reluctantly. Tranquilizers, as far as I was concerned, weren't the answer, only another problem. I had memories of the days when I was expecting Joy.

Within a few days I was fighting the familiar depression and lethargy. The mental struggle of whether to take the pills or not only increased my misery. I couldn't go on like this. Alan and I prayed and decided to call the doctor. I told him that I couldn't take the tranquilizers any longer and that I would look to the Lord for healing and strength. To my relief, he was most understanding.

On returning from ministering at a Charismatic conference in Fiji, Alan found an invitation waiting for him. The Second International Leaders Conference, organized by the

International Catholic Charismatic Renewal Services, was to be held in Rome in May 1975. Ten Protestant observers from around the world had been invited and Alan was one of them. I had been invited to attend as well.

We prayed and submitted the idea to our recently formed Board of Directors. They agreed that Alan should go to Rome. It would be valuable experience for him and for the ministry. Alan believed I should go too, but I needed health and money.

I had already unexpectedly received $400 for my personal needs from Pastor Peter Morrow in New Zealand a few weeks earlier. At the time, I had wondered what to use it for. Now I knew. The return fare to Rome was far more than $400, but we remembered my brother David at Qantas. We called and found to our delight that I could purchase a concession ticket to Rome for exactly $400.

All I needed now was the strength. I began to claim restoration and to resist pain and weakness. I improved gradually over the next six weeks and by the day of departure I was strong enough to travel.

One thing still concerned me. This was my first trip overseas without Beth or Joy and the first time I had been away for Mother's Day. I was sure God wanted me to go and I trusted Him to undertake for the separation, but it was still heartrending. After we dropped Beth and Joy at Mum and Dad's in Gosford north of Sydney, I cried for the first two miles along the road.

I would have been even more upset if I had know what happened an hour later when Dad took Beth and Joy for a walk. A large dog ran out and attacked Beth, biting her on her hip and leaving a hole in her yellow skirt. She had to go to the hospital for a tetanus injection. The devil was obviously not happy about our trip to Rome and as often happens before major trips, the family was attacked. Mum and Dad thought it best to keep the news of the attack from us and we left the next day thinking all was well.

Rome was a city with an atmosphere and character all its own. We discovered in the cab ride from the airport to the hotel that there were no apparent rules of the road. The Italians drove as though they were going to die tomorrow. They kept one hand on the horn and one foot on the accelerator. During the frequent traffic jams, they resorted to yelling at one another. If it was traumatic being a cab passenger, it was even worse being a pedestrian. We heard that, supposedly, the best way to cross the road in Rome was to put your head in a newspaper and step off the curb. We never had the courage to try it!

Our hotel was a modest one several stories high. The manager booked us in, carried our bags, worked the antiquated elevator and served our meals. Maybe he cooked as well, we thought, as we watched him change roles all the time. We were given a room—the honeymoon suite, in fact—with shutters and its own bathroom. We discovered that this was a luxury compared to other rooms, even though water took ages to go down the drain.

Brian Smith and several other Australian Catholic Charismatic leaders were booked into the same hotel. We went out to dinner as a group. One man ordered a dish from the menu that turned out to be fried seaweed. We played it safe and ordered something we understood—spaghetti. The Australian group also provided some laughs back at the hotel. One of them visited the bathroom late at night, went to open the door and found that the doorknob came away in his hand. No one heard his cries for help and there he sat until someone eventually came to his rescue.

Life in Rome wasn't always so amusing. I made the mistake of drinking several glasses of tap water one night when I was thirsty. I found out the next day just how much of a mistake it was when I developed diarrhea and vomiting. I was still sick by the time we moved to a monastery-like villa for the Leaders' Conference. I carried a box of crackers and a bottle of pop everywhere I went. My back was painful. The bed was too soft, so we put our suitcases underneath it to hold it up. I was so sick that I had to rest, which was frustrating, seeing I had come all this way to be part of the conference. I was given some pills, but they didn't help. I was sitting at one meal, feeling nauseous just looking at the oily green beans on my plate, when Brian Smith provided the scriptural remedy. "Why don't you take a little wine for your stomach's sake? The doctor in Australia told me wine kills the germs in the food."

We came from a Methodist temperance background and alcohol was taboo, but I was so sick I was willing to try anything. So I began to have half an inch of wine at meals. I couldn't stand the taste—so much for my old fear that I could be a potential alcoholic if I ever drank. Alan took the same remedy for his mildly upset stomach. Much to my relief, I was soon feeling better.

The Lord spoke to Alan through this experience. "You have always expected them to change to be like you, but all of you have to change to be like Me."

Alan realized that unity would not come through one church conforming to another, but all churches changing into the image of Christ. It wasn't only our upset stomachs that were healed, but our narrow-mindedness. Interestingly enough, on our return to Australia, we discovered that the Methodist Church had revoked its anti-alcohol laws.

About 250 Catholic leaders from all around the world had come together. The small group of Protestant observers included David du Plessis, Terry Fullam, Larry Christianson from America, Michael Harper from England, and Derek Crumptom from South Africa. Alan was honored to represent Australia.

We met every day for worship and prayer and to hear reports on Catholic Renewal worldwide. One report in particular impressed me. A leader from Ireland, Cecil Kerr, told us of the suffering and persecution, the fighting between the Catholics and the Protestants, and how Christian faith was growing strong in the midst of it. He related how Christian Protestants and Catholics risked their lives to meet together for prayer, their love and unity a dramatic contrast to the hatred and violence all around them. Toward the end of the Leaders Conference, two Protestants, Larry Christianson and Alan, were each asked to share for ten minutes, which was quite a privilege.

The most memorable time for me was the Eucharist Celebration. As Protestants, we were not allowed to receive the elements, and we chose two seats at the back of the auditorium. The worship time was full of the songs I enjoyed. The Catholic songs had a unique, often minor-keyed style. As people began to file forward to receive communion, we were singing about being one in the Spirit and one Body. The realization hit me that in reality, the words of the song were not true—we were a divided Body. I began to weep as a well of emotion sprang up from deep inside. I knew the tears were not because I felt left out. I was feeling the burden of the Lord, seeing His Body divided and broken instead of united.

I couldn't control my sobs. They poured out in great waves of grief. I was embarrassed, but there was nothing I could do about it. I was glad to be at the back of the room.

Several of the Australian Catholics saw me crying and gathered around as the song continued. One of them put his arms around me and said softly, "Will you forgive us?" I couldn't talk through my sobs. They prayed quietly, showing their love and concern. I was still crying after they finished praying, and I blurted out to Alan, "I think the Holy Spirit is interceding through me and perhaps I should find a quieter place."

I left the auditorium, sobbing, and crossed the courtyard to a small chapel. I went in, grateful to find it deserted, and sank to my knees in one of the front pews. Agonizing sobs came forth from the depths of my being. I felt as though my heart was breaking. Words in other tongues poured from my mouth as I cried out to the Lord.

Through the sobs and tears I began to express what was on my heart. "Jesus prayed that they may all be one, Father. *'May they be one, so that the world will believe that You sent Me. I gave them the same glory You gave Me, so that they may be one, just as You and I are one. I in them and You in Me, so that they may be completely one,'" (John 17:21-23 Good News For Modern Man).*

If Jesus had prayed for unity then it had to happen. God would certainly answer the prayer of Jesus. But even as I was speaking, Satan seemed to respond in my ear. "Has God said this would be? The church is never going to be one Body. It's impossible. There is too much division. It can never happen. Don't believe it."

I could almost hear the sneering tone of his voice as he tempted me to disbelieve the prayer of Jesus. Instead, I felt faith and authority rise within me and found myself answering, "Yes, surely God has said we are one Body in Christ. Jesus has prayed the will of God, that we may be one. Surely His Father has heard and answered that prayer. Is anything too hard for the Lord? Hallelujah!"

I rose from my knees and went out into the bright sunlight, still crying. In the garden outside the chapel, a tremendous peace came. I knew that Protestants, Catholics, the whole Body would be united and I would see it happen according to Jesus' prayer in John 17.

Nearby were cages of lovebirds and white doves, a reminder that both the love and the power of the Holy Spirit would bring this about. I took a pen and wrote down what God was speaking to my heart.

"Truly," says the Lord, "I will give you a new heart, My Body, My flesh; partake of it. You all are My Body, all who believe in Me are in Me, abiding in Me. Don't you see that to partake of My Body you must partake of all of My Body? I am the bread of life. I have given My Body to be broken that each of you might have life in yourselves, but only as you gather the fragments will the whole loaf become one. Despise not the crumbs, are they not part of the loaf?"

My prayer and intercession began to bear fruit the next day. We were invited to lunch with all the Australian leaders, who were discussing plans for Catholic Renewal in Australia. They had planned a yearly conference in Brisbane, the next one set for July 1976. But instead of another in July 1977, Brian Smith suggested they combine with The Temple Trust conference in January 1977. He asked Alan if he would be willing to organize the conference for them. Alan readily agreed to do so. It would be his honor and privilege. A joint Catholic/Protestant conference would be history-making for Australia. It would play a significant role in the fulfillment of my prayers, at least as far as the church in Australia was concerned. It was clearly evident that it was part of God's plan to bring unity in the Body of Christ.

That Sunday was Mother's Day and Alan wanted to buy me some momento from Rome as a gift. I knew what God wanted me to have—a cross on a chain. I remembered that as a child, I had often pleaded with my mother to buy me a little cross to wear. We had friends who were jewelers and I used to stare longingly at the different crosses through the shop window. Each one reminded me of Jesus and His love for me.

Mum would always say, "No, a cross is Catholic."

It was so Catholic that we couldn't have anything to do with it. Even a cross in a church created a stir with many Protestants, and I grew up afraid to wear a cross.

So it was with mixed feelings that I looked at all the crosses. There were plenty of them for sale at the conference, so many that it was impossible to choose one. It wasn't until we visited the Coliseum that I knew I would find my cross. This was the right place, where men and women had given up their lives for their faith and shed their blood, even as Jesus had done.

Alan bought me a simple gold cross, etched with tiny fishes, from one of the many merchants. It cost only a dollar, but to me it was priceless. I took it back to Australia and as I began to wear it, God healed me of the childhood apprehension. Now I wear it frequently.

The Leaders Conference was over, and we moved back to the hotel for the main conference. Though we had a busy schedule we did find time to have lunch at a quaint sidewalk cafe. We visited the famous Tivoli Fountain and from there we took a ride through the streets and parks of Rome in an open carriage drawn by a white horse. It was an unforgettable experience.

Our hotel was in an excellent location in the heart of the city. From there we would travel each day by bus to join 10,000 other Christians at a 2000-year old meeting place, the Catacombs. The grassy area above the tombs became an open-air auditorium. Tents became meeting rooms. There were not enough portable toilets and the lines of people stretched hundreds of yards. People waited patiently, or not so patiently, in what seemed like an impossible situation.

The first afternoon offered a choice of workshops. Alan went off to one while I wandered around, not sure where God wanted me to go. Along one of the tree-lined walkways I came across a large, open-air gathering. I could see a figure on the distant platform, a very tall man in white flowing robes. His face was too far away to be distinct, but as I listened to him, the love and the presence of Jesus struck me with an intensity I had never before felt. It was as if Jesus himself was there in front of the crowd. I discovered the man's name was Francis McNutt. And I told Alan excitedly, "You have to invite that man to come and speak in Australia."

The Conference was alive with many different songs, languages and people, and full of powerful worship and ministry. At one point, the Holy Spirit came across the great crowd in a visible way accompanied by an audible wave of spontaneous praise as people raised their hands and voices to the Lord.

One afternoon during free time, we left the green fields sprinkled with scarlet poppies, the blue sky and warm sunshine, and went down into the Catacombs. They were the underground tombs where the early Christians had found refuge during Roman persecution. Their fish symbols were still etched in the ancient stone walls. It was strange to be in that place of death, which had served as a place of fellowship, acutely aware of the gathering of Christians above us who were free to worship the Lord and openly fellowship together.

The finale of our stay in Rome was a visit to Saint Peter's Basilica on Pentecost Sunday. This was Holy Year and it must have been a thrilling experience for a Catholic to be in Rome for such an occasion. Fifty thousand people crowded in and around the cathedral. There were no seats and the crowd stood crammed shoulder-to-shoulder on the marble floor. The only space in the entire building was the center aisle.

As part of the international delegation we received preferential treatment. We were admitted at a side entrance by guards in colorful uniforms and given purple-cushioned seats at the front of the church.

I was moved by the reverence and respect the people displayed for their leader. As the Pope was carried down the aisle they acclaimed him with shouts of joy. Behind us a girl fainted, overcome with excitement. This certainly was a once-in-a-lifetime experience and I could understand their emotion.

The Pope's address on the joy of the Holy Spirit was followed by the Eucharist. This time, Australian Catholic priests urged us to take part. It was with great reverence that I stepped forward to receive that wafer on my tongue, aware of the tremendous privilege of tasting the unity that God had promised.

We wondered how we would ever get through the crowd at the close of the service. We had been introduced to film star Loretta Young's husband and he took our hands and told us, "Hold on. Follow me and I'll get you through."

The square outside St. Peter's was as crowded as the basilica itself. We could hardly glimpse the cobblestones. As far as we could see, from the steps of St. Peter's to the semi-circle of arches and pillars, were throngs of people.

We were booked on a flight leaving Rome the next morning. The airport, still troubled with strikes, had an uneasy atmosphere to say the least. The man behind the ticket counter glared at us, took one look at my concession ticket, and said, "You won't be able to get on this flight."

Our names were clearly written on the list in front of him and we must have looked as puzzled as we felt.

He said flatly, "You are not listed."

"But my name is on the list," I protested.

He snapped back, "It isn't there now!" And he put a line through my name.

"What are we supposed to do now?" we asked.

"Get a later flight," he told us impatiently.

We explained that we had to make the connection in Amsterdam, or we had no way of getting home. He was unmoved and more irritable than ever. As far as he was concerned we weren't going and that was that.

We picked up our bags and retreated out of earshot, but not out of sight. We began to pray, rebuking the enemy and thanking the Lord that He would make a way where there was no way. Half an hour later, the man beckoned us back.

He said almost apologetically, "You can go now."

He had reinserted our names on the list. We praised God all the way to the plane.

Using my concession ticket meant that we had to fly for hours in the wrong direction back to Amsterdam, and then 27 hours on to Australia. The more than 30-hour flight was the longest in our experience and the most agonizing for me. With every landing and takeoff, my ears grew more and more painful. Alan and I spent most of that flight in prayer. I also read a book called *The Christian's Secret of a Happy Life*, by

Hannah Whitehall Smith. She wrote of circumstances as chariots of God that lift us to a higher place of maturity and knowing God. I certainly clung to God on that trip.

By the time we landed in Sydney I was almost deaf.

We were reunited with our daughters, and my hearing gradually returned to normal. Not all was well, however. We found the ministry staff undermined and divided. They were split into two camps—one supporting Alan and me and the other at odds with us. The air was full of criticism, bitterness and disloyalty. It became obvious that while we were in Rome, the enemy had taken the opportunity to sow seeds of disunity in the ministry.

In the confrontation that followed, half the staff and some of the board members left the ministry. It was a painful, but necessary discipline and chastening. We came through the refiner's fire smaller in number, but stronger in commitment to Him, to each other, and to the work He had called us to do.

Two years later, in January 1977, the prayers and plans that were fashioned in Rome came to fruition before our very eyes. The Catholic Charismatics had their conference from Friday night through Sunday morning, with Francis McNutt as the featured speaker. At their request, The Temple Trust handled all the organization for their conference. Jeff Lawrence, a Catholic Charismatic, joined our staff and became a liaison with the Catholic Charismatic leaders, including Brian Smith of Brisbane.

The International Conference on the Holy Spirit and the Church, sponsored by The Temple Trust, was held from that Sunday to the following Friday night. Altogether, it was a powerful, unforgettable week.

The days prior to the conference were hectic. Many volunteered to help, but in the now-cramped quarters of the office at 151 Clovelly Road, just finding a place for them to work was a challenge. So, anywhere they could find a spare corner, even up the stairways, people could be found, sorting through files, recording registrations, typing name tags, answering inquiries and trying to solve the inevitable problems that arose, such as accommodation muddles and wrong registrations. There seemed to be no end to it.

With over 5,000 registrations and 15 international speakers billed, it was the biggest task The Temple Trust had ever handled. Yet, through all the hard work, and despite the heat wave conditions that preceded the Conference, a real sense of joy and expectation permeated the gathering. God was going to do something great at this conference that Australia had never before seen. Even though workers staggered home at four o'clock in the morning on the day the Conference started, their sense of excitement had not diminished.

The highlight of the conference was undoubtedly the Thursday night meeting in the Horden Pavilion at which Reverend Tommy Tyson, a Methodist minister, and Father Francis McNutt, a Dominican priest, both from America, shared in an unforgettable act of reconciliation. Standing in as representatives for their respective traditions and kneeling together on the platform, they confessed the sins and wrong attitudes that had existed through the centuries between Catholics and Protestants, going back even as far as the Spanish Inquisition.

As I watched through tear-filled eyes, and listened to the heartfelt words and prayers, my heart was overwhelmed with a deep sense of gratitude to God. This was truly holy ground. I felt both humbled and honored to be present at such a significant gathering.

The presence of the Holy Spirit was so powerful that night that it could practically be felt as liquid love flowing among the 6,000 people that were present. As Tommy Tyson's and Francis MacNutt's prayers became a reality in people's hearts, long-held prejudices and barriers simply melted away. Then, as Protestant ministers and Catholic priests partnered together and went out in pairs to minister to the people, a fresh river of healing began to flow. It was certainly a night to remember, and was etched deeply into our hearts and minds.

Sitting on the platform that night, my thoughts inevitably went back to all that had happened in Rome two years earlier. I recalled the tears of intercession for unity in the Body of Christ, the travail, the struggle with Satan in the chapel, and the prayer of Jesus—*"That they may be one..."*

Incredible as it seemed, those prayers were being answered right before my eyes. *"To God be the glory for the things He has done!"*

CHAPTER 21

An Unexpected Promotion

"Enlarge the place of your tent, and let them
stretch out the curtains of your dwellings.
Do not spare, lengthen your cords."
Isaiah 54:2

"I want a Bible college like this in Australia," was the word Murray Cameron distinctly heard from the Lord while visiting Faith Bible College in New Zealand in May 1975. This was not a brand new idea to Murray, the pastor of Southside Christian Fellowship in Sydney. The vision for a Bible college had been burning in his heart for 18 years.

On his return from New Zealand, Murray invited some interested Christian leaders over to his apartment to share his vision. Altogether, six men gathered for that first meeting—Keith Browning, Gordon Gibbs, Paul Grant, Charles Widdowson, Alan, and Murray Cameron. It was shocking weather that afternoon. As Alan drove to the meeting through torrential rain, a gust of wind blew the top vent off of our camper van.

Dripping wet, the men crowded into the Cameron's front room and Murray began to share his vision. Nothing could dampen their enthusiasm. Each had an immediate leap of excitement in his spirit. Yes, this was what God wanted in Australia.

They set another meeting for June. As many of their wives were involved in a ladies meeting at Pitt Street Congregational Church where Dick Mills was speaking, the men decided to hold their meeting at the same time in a back room. By this stage, Don Baker had joined the group. At that meeting they agreed, as a step of faith, to open a bank account and each put down a deposit of ten dollars. They also arranged to send out a leaflet advertising the start of the college the following year, in February 1976. The school was to be called Vision Bible College, based on Habakkuk 2:2-3, *"Write the vision and make it plain on tablets, that he may run who reads it."*

Later that same week, Murray was attending a Temple Trust minister's conference where Dick Mills was the speaker. Dick was ministering prophetically to the individual men row by row, beginning at the front. Murray was sitting in one of the back rows. It was 12:12 p.m. and he had to leave at 12:15 to keep another appointment, when suddenly, for no apparent reason, Dick reversed his order and began ministering from the back.

He called Murray forward and gave him a list of scriptures, all of which had to do with "vision," including the very verse from which Vision Bible College got its name—Habakkuk 2. Then Dick started to prophesy: "That which has been on your heart for 18 years will come to pass in six months." He knew nothing of the plans for Vision Bible College!

Despite this incredible confirmation, the testing was far from over. The college was due to start in February, but by

November, they still didn't have a principal or suitable venue. A further meeting was called to discuss the matter.

At the time, The Temple Trust was negotiating to obtain "Hebron," Youth With A Mission's former Australian headquarters in the Eastern Suburbs of Sydney, with a goal of setting up a community center there. We had been meeting monthly with a small group of pastors from the Eastern Suburbs. We all agreed that it would be good to have a center for ministry and community activities. Alan had the idea of putting a preschool daycare in the large rooms at the front of the house, with the rest of it being used for community activities. We had spent quite some time poring over a floor plan of the house, trying to allocate different rooms to various needs. Every time Alan mentioned the preschool I felt uneasy. I didn't think it was right to put it there and I couldn't explain why.

While Alan was away meeting with the other men to discuss the need for a principal and venue for the Bible college, I was doing the washing. It was a sunny day and I enjoyed the comfortable warmth as I hung out the washing in our tiny back garden in Bronte Road. I reached up to put clothespins on the line and all of a sudden a thought came into my mind. It seemed as though God was saying to me, "You know about the preschool. You know you are right about it not going into Hebron."

I felt reassured.

"If the preschool is not to take up that space then you realize something else has to fit into the plan."

Well, that's logical, I thought, not expecting what was to follow.

"You, Alan and the girls will be living there instead."

I was momentarily stunned. But I knew that I had heard from God. Our little backyard garden became holy ground. I couldn't wait until Alan came home to tell him what God had said to me.

Meanwhile, the Bible college meeting had no sooner been underway than the Lord began to reveal the missing pieces of the jigsaw puzzle. Hebron wasn't for a community center but for Vision Bible College. It was to come under the umbrella of The Temple Trust's ministry, Alan was to be the principal, and he and his family were to live there. In 20 minutes the whole thing had fallen into place.

Alan returned home, wondering how he was going to break the news to me, not knowing God had already prepared me for it.

I had seen Hebron a few times before. One Thursday night I had attended a crowded prayer fellowship meeting held by YWAM, then the owners of the house. I didn't recall much except the tattered blue carpet, the warm fellowship and Dean Sherman's teaching. Of course, I never thought I would be living there. Alan had taken me to look at the outside when we were thinking of it for a community center. On previous visits I hadn't taken much notice of the details. Now, my situation had changed. I was going to live in it.

The original owner must have been someone of considerable means. Situated on a corner, Hebron was a gracious, old, cream-painted home with high ceilings, built in the Victorian era. Its wide verandas and bay window in the large dining room faced east. From the vantage point on the hill there must have been a commanding view of the Pacific Ocean, the headland, and the sandy shoreline known as Coogee Beach. It was the kind of house that one imagined with spacious grounds, shady trees, and a long, curving driveway.

Instead, there was a short path flanked by two very old palm trees, which provided housing for numerous sparrows.

The verandas were now filled in and little remained of the surrounding property or the view. All one could see now were the red tile roofs of houses and the numerous high-rise apartments that covered every available land space. One small patch of deep blue that could be seen between the houses was the only reminder that the Pacific Ocean was a few minutes away.

We were both excited to recognize God's call to lead the Bible college. I must confess I did experience some apprehension. At the beginning of the year the Lord had said "Go, shut thyself in thine house." It had been good to have times alone and quiet periods of undisturbed fellowship with the Lord. That luxury was soon to be threatened. Besides, I was physically weary and just to imagine living in a big house with a crowd of students was quite a challenge. I couldn't help thinking back to 1971. A flood of memories began to fill my mind as I began to recall those years at Lugar Brae.

Now, five years later and a little wiser, it seemed God was giving us another opportunity to be involved in community life. It would not have been my choice at the time, but it was quite clear God had arranged it. That was sufficient for me. He would surely enable me to cope somehow, proving Himself faithful to us and our family. I was reminded of a remarkable occasion 12 months earlier when God had chosen to say to our family, "I love you, I am with you and I will take care of all your needs." He had done this by answering our prayers for help in a spectacular way.

It was November the 29th, our wedding anniversary. I had been upstairs in the big old house on Bronte Road. I had cleared the breakfast dishes and the girls were at school. It was

Friday, I hadn't been shopping yet, and our food supply was very low. We were down to salt, pepper, a handful of corn flakes, and next to nothing in the fridge. I called Alan at the office.

"Do you have any money, yet?" I asked. "Has anyone given you any? I don't have any money to buy food and nothing has come in the mail today."

"Sorry, I don't have any either," Alan answered. "We don't have any at home, anywhere at all?"

"Well, the girls do have about ten dollars in their piggy bank, but we don't feel right about touching that. I guess we will just wait and see what happens."

We were not on a salary, but were living by faith. Our only option was to trust God, pray, and wait.

It was now three in the afternoon and I still hadn't been shopping, and it was almost time for the girls to come home from school. There was a knock on the front door. I could see the shape of someone through the old stained glass. It couldn't be Beth or Joy, as they would not be knocking. There were voices, too, but they were not clearly recognizable. I opened the door and was surprised to see a couple who lived in Wollongong, two hours drive south of Sydney.

"Hello, come in," I said, wondering why they had dropped in today.

"Well, actually we have something for you." They pointed to their big station wagon parked at the curb. Now I was curious. They obviously wanted me to follow them out to the car. They led the way to the back of the station wagon, put the key in the lock and lifted the hatch. It was packed with boxes and bags of all sizes, with stuff jammed in every available space. I looked and began to realize it was filled with groceries. I stared at it, not being able to figure out what was going on.

"It's for you," they said. "We argued with the Lord about bringing all this food on a Friday. We were sure you would have already been shopping, but the Lord said this morning to bring it and reassured us that you have not been shopping. So, here we are. We hope you need it."

Then it dawned on me! This whole station wagon was full of groceries for us. God had sent this dear couple with His provision. Now I understood why no money had come in and why I could not go shopping. God wanted to do something very special.

They began carrying the bags and boxes up the stairs to our kitchen. What I thought was a mountain of provisions in the station wagon now turned into an avalanche and spread everywhere in the kitchen and living/dining room. Counters, tables, chairs, and the floor were all covered. Beth and Joy arrived home in the middle of it all and their eyes widened with wonder and excitement to see God's bountiful provision.

There was everything we could ever need and more, from dairy, meat, fruit, cans, and bread, to toilet paper and paper towels, napkins and paper plates—everything. It was more than we would ever buy for ourselves, both basics and special treats.

As we unpacked, they said excitedly, "We had wanted to bring this three weeks ago when we had an appointment to see Alan, but that was postponed at the last minute. So, we bought all the non-perishables and had packed them, continuing to ask God if we could bring it. Each time God said, 'No, wait.'"

That Friday morning God had finally said, "Today's the day."

Obeying orders, but still apprehensive about it being Friday, they went off to buy all the perishable foods—eggs, milk, meat, fruit, vegetables—and, as an after-thought, added a fruit cake. They didn't know it was our wedding anniversary nor did they know we had no money for groceries. But God knew. Now they knew as well, and were so blessed to be an answer to prayer that was right on time.

After they left, Beth, Joy and I went excitedly from box to box. It was like Christmas, full of surprises and exclamations of delight as we unpacked the contents. With great joy we put everything away, filling empty cupboards to overflowing. The laundry had to become a storage room. It was like having our own shop at home.

The first thing we did was to give a tithe of it away to other people. What a celebration we had together that night as, with gratitude, we sat around the table eating the food God had so lovingly supplied.

I felt reassured as I recalled the reality of God's amazing care in the details and timing of His provision. He knew what was ahead of us now. He would take care of us.

Time was short. We were to open the college at the end of January 1976. There were Christmas celebrations and also major conferences to be held in Adelaide and Brisbane during January. We needed a miracle to be ready on time.

Then came the mad dash, painting and pulling down walls to make an apartment in the front of the house for our family. New carpet was laid throughout the apartment and down the long, wide hall. Floor tiles were still being laid in the kitchen at 2 a.m. the day of the opening service. The first students to arrive were rather surprised to find their rooms empty, even more surprised when they were given their first job—assembling their own beds.

For the first week, Alan slept on the floor while the rubble was being cleared from our small apartment. It consisted of two small bedrooms for Beth and Joy (still under construction), a living/dining room, and an area for a kitchen and bathroom (which were not yet in existence). A large bedroom with a bay window was on the other side of the house across the hall.

This was not ideal, but would have to work for Alan and me. I recalled something Edith Schaeffer had written: *"A family is an open door with hinges and a lock."* We would put double doors across the wide hall that would stand open during the day, but closed at night to give our family some privacy.

At the grand opening service, it was my honor and joy to cut the ribbon across the front door of Vision Bible College, our new home. The dedication was conducted by Jim Glennon, from St. Andrew's Cathedral in Sydney, and the message by Des Short, principal of Faith Bible College in New Zealand. God had been faithful. He had provided everything except for one very important thing—a cook.

This had been a special prayer concern for me. Every time the subject came up, people looked at me. "You will do the cooking, of course," they said.

"No," I replied emphatically, "I won't be cooking. I believe God will provide someone else to cook for the college."

Inside I felt peace about that. I had experience cooking for a large household but I knew God didn't want me to do it for Vision Bible College. At times I felt I was the only one who thought that. Even on opening day, showing people through the gracious old house, when we came to the large kitchen with the big wooden table in the middle of the room they would say, "You'll be doing the cooking, won't you?" Each time I would politely say no, someone else will.

Alan had a phone call from John Ollis, an Assembly of God pastor from the north side of the city who had been at the opening service and who had heard Alan's plea for a cook. He had a young man in his church who was a cook and was interested in a job in a Christian environment. One problem was the distance. Nevertheless, the appointment for the job interview was made.

Ian Bartley was on his way to The Temple Trust office intending to tell Alan he didn't want this particular job when, within a few yards of the office, the Lord apprehended him and told him he was to do it. After the interview he walked down to the college to have a look at the place and in particular, the kitchen.

That was where I first met him, a tall, auburn-haired young man with a soft-spoken voice and a New Zealand accent. He was dressed in blue jeans and a white shirt. He started work two weeks later and came in five days a week to cook lunches and dinner and also prepare food for the weekends. Ian proved to be a tremendous asset to the college, not only for his culinary expertise, but also for the rich contribution he made spiritually to the lives of those whom he served.

In that first intake there were only ten students, six men and four women, representing several denominations, including Catholic and Protestant. The Lord was certainly drawing his people together.

I found myself in the midst of a community again. Seven days a week, 24 hours a day.

CHAPTER 22

A Living School Room

*"Come, and let us go up to the mountain of the
Lord, to the house of the God of Jacob. He will
teach us His ways, and we shall walk in His paths."*
Isaiah 2:3

"This is my golden opportunity," I said excitedly. "I have
always wanted to go to Bible college and now my dream can
come true." Each day for three weeks I hurried through my
early morning chores and made sure Beth and Joy were off to
school. I would throw my clothes on, grab my Bible and
notebook and race down the hall into the lecture room, slipping
quietly into the seat by the door. After classes and lunch with
the students, I would attend to all my other chores as well as
oversee the running of the household.

One morning, while making my usual mad dash down the
hall, pulling my sweater round my shoulders while at the same
time trying not to drop my Bible and books, I stopped short in
the middle of the hall. It seemed God was saying, "Do you
really think this is what I want you to be doing?"

I stood still for a moment like a statue, a sinking feeling
invading my heart. Then I realized the truth. I was the one who

wanted to go to Bible college classes. I had assumed this was God's opportunity for me, that He wanted it, too. I realized He had been patiently waiting these last three weeks for me to stop long enough to ask Him. I turned around and walked slowly back up the hall to our living room.

"Alright God, I know you want me to give up the idea of going to classes. I realize I can't keep up the hectic pace and look after my family properly at the same time." I was disappointed but I knew it was right. My life as a college student was over. It was only a short time, however, before I was asked to begin lecturing the students. I taught a series on Christian Growth and Maturity.

Classes were held Tuesday through Friday mornings and some afternoons. The students were rostered to clean the house and work in the garden. They were also expected to help prepare the food for meals, serve and wash up. Some of them had never peeled a potato, washed a dish, or made a bed before coming to college, let alone cleaned a toilet, an oven or a refrigerator. It brought out various reactions and attitudes. What they couldn't do they learned to do, and after awhile acceptance came, and routines went smoothly.

Meals were always a highlight in the college program, and Ian took very good care of us all. Luscious Australian Pavlovas topped with cream and Kiwi fruit or strawberries, were always the most popular treat for dessert. As the student body grew, it became quite a regular occurrence to have 60 or more people at dinner, including staff and guests.

Each Sunday after church, I cooked dinner in the college kitchen for all the members of the household. Beth would play her guitar and as the students came home they all crowded into the kitchen. It was great to have a sing-along while enjoying the delicious aromas. We set aside Saturdays and one evening each week especially for our family, and another evening to share a family night with the students. These special times proved invaluable for our relationships.

I enjoyed my role as principal's wife, at least most of the time. To the students I became a kind of "mother" and found plenty of opportunities to give advice, love and encouragement. The hardest part for me was giving correction. Alan was at the office or frequently away ministering, so I couldn't avoid this responsibility. I would die a thousand deaths and rehearse what I would say whenever I had to confront someone. I hated doing it but knew God was developing my character and leadership ability through such experiences.

Sometimes I would cry out to God and say, "Why did you put someone like me in a position of leadership?"

I would always have to come back to the fact that Alan and I were called and appointed by God and He must have thought we were the right people for the job. In the process, I also learned that students, like children, responded to a balance of love and discipline.

One way the Lord developed my leadership ability and provided training for the students was through Children's Bible Club. This was a midweek outreach ministry to up to a hundred children that we held at the Lugar Brae church hall. Vision students took turns as part of a ministry team for six weeks. As a result, they learned to communicate Bible truths in a very simple and practical way. Some who objected to taking part, later found themselves called to full-time children's ministry.

Bible Club was a blessing for Beth and Joy also. Beth's skills were developed in music and drama preparation, and Joy received the benefit of learning and taking part with all the children.

At times I found myself with the dilemma of switching roles from wife and mother to principal's wife, lecturer and counselor. Most of the time the family functioned well, although Beth found it difficult to settle down to homework and study, especially during the first year. What teenager would want to be shut away in her room with schoolbooks when there was a house full of young people always doing something that made for fun and fellowship? In fact, certain students would come and knock on our door in the evening and ask if Beth could come and play Monopoly. She always provided a challenge and some stiff competition. Joy loved the community too, but had a bit more difficulty when she would get so attached to students that her heart would break when it was time for them to leave.

Actually, I had to make major adjustments myself. I can still remember the time Beth, Joy and I said goodbye to the first group of students. Alan was away that weekend. We went to the front door with each student as they left. We hugged each one. It was traumatic, like saying goodbye to family. Tears rolled down our cheeks. Finally, the old front door was closed as the last student drove away and we turned and walked across the tiled porch and down the huge hallway. We were alone.

The big old house seemed so quiet and empty now. The only sounds were our own sobs as we comforted each other. I didn't think I would ever get over it. Another group of students would arrive to take their place in the next intake. I didn't think it possible for me to love them in the same way. God showed me I could choose to harden my heart to protect myself from being hurt again, or I could allow Him to enlarge my heart to love the second group of new students just as much as I had loved the first. I chose to have Him enlarge my heart of love.

Over the years that followed, my heart enlarged many times to include many, many, spiritual sons and daughters.

Not only did I grow in my ability to love others, but while at Hebron I came to a deeper revelation and acceptance of God's love for me.

There were several advantages to a residential-style college. One was the fact that because there was a day after day exposure to each other in close living situations, there was little time to hide. At first, of course, everyone was on their best behavior, but usually after about a month of intensive community living, the masks people wore began to come off. The rubbing together of one person's temperament with another had the same effect as sandpaper. In fact, all of us had to undergo "the sandpaper treatment."

From seeing all the faults in everyone else, the Lord had to bring us to see the faults in ourselves. The positive things and the gifts had to be brought out and developed also. This wasn't always easy for some people. One girl was so nervous about having to give a five-minute testimony on weekend ministry at a church that she planned to run away. She wasn't the only one. Quite a few thought about escape when the going was tough. It was really hard for some students to allow God to work through difficult and painful things in their lives.

Bringing men and women of different ages, backgrounds, temperaments, and church traditions together, and mixing them up in ministry situations, living circumstances, and relationships, provided a crucible in which God could begin His refining process. Praise God, not one student was lost during the time in college.

The work to which Alan and I were called, renewal and restoration, working towards unity in the whole Body of

Christ, was of course a strong influence in the life of Vision Bible College. Alan arranged the lecture schedules and had a significant input into the classes. He arranged for the students to be exposed to lecturers from many different backgrounds and points of view. Many of the speakers we brought in for conferences also ministered at the college and spent time in fellowship over meals and conversation with the students. A great deal of faith and vision was imparted at such times. There is nothing quite like sitting down to a cup of tea or coffee and talking one-on-one with great men and women of God. Finding out they were human like everyone else was a revelation for some students.

It was just as well that God enlarged my heart to receive and love the second intake of students, because out of that group God had prepared some very special people who were to be a part of our lives and ministry for a number of years. We had taken the students away for a weekend to "Orana Lodge," our retreat house at McMasters Beach. It was Saturday night and Alan was tired and wanted to get to bed, but God had something else in mind. After an evening of sharing together we all joined hands in the living room to pray. We realized God had bonded us together in a special way. Instead of being called to something else after college, several students felt called to remain with us in the ministry. Thus, The Temple Trust Task Force was born.

This was a dedicated, committed, small team of people sacrificially serving Alan and me and the ministry. They were given room and food, but had to look to the Lord for everything else. It was a living schoolroom of faith. Each person, gifted in their own areas, put their hands to anything. Their help was a tremendous support and blessing.

It wasn't all hard work, though. There was a lot of fun and many ministry opportunities, too. One of the great, memorable, fun experiences was a video on Vision Bible College produced by the Task Force under the directorship of Syd Polley, who later worked in the television ministry of Hillsong Church in Sydney. Lynette Maxwell was another one who became one of our administrators and later organized John Wimber's conferences in Australia for Dan Armstrong.

Within a year or two we were in need of more space for more students. The decision was made to employ a builder to put another story on Hebron. Plans were drawn for an attic dormitory and the work was scheduled to be completed over the Christmas summer break.

This was going to be a busy time for the ministry, as we also had five conferences over four weeks all over Australia, from Townsville in the north, to Melbourne and Hobart in the south, and from Canberra across to Perth in Western Australia. In the midst of this somewhat chaotic time, we received the news that the city council would not approve any addition to the building. Our reaction to this news was, "God, what are you going to do now?"

When Alan returned from the last conference, we faced the inevitable crisis over where to put all the incoming students. Alan gathered the staff together in his office and read the story of Moses and the crossing of the Red Sea in Exodus chapter 14, and declared the word, "Stand still and see the salvation of God." Just like Moses, but on a smaller scale, we needed a miracle.

Mary, a member of our Task Force, knew someone in the Catholic Charismatic Renewal ministry and told him about our dilemma. He knew of a big Catholic convent only a short distance away from Hebron, and some of the nuns attended his prayer meetings. Perhaps they could help. It was the

Wednesday before the students' arrival date and inquiries were made on our behalf. Good news; they were willing to talk to us and at least discuss our situation.

The day came for the students to arrive and still we had nowhere to house them. They crowded into the dining room with their bags and expected to be allocated to a room. We gave a brief explanation about what had happened, how our plans to enlarge the building had not been approved, but reassured them that the Lord would provide.

It was Friday morning and Alan and I went to the convent for an 11 a.m. appointment and were given a tour of inspection by one of the sisters. It was a large, two-story property in a choice position on a hill overlooking the Pacific Ocean. There were meeting rooms, a prayer chapel, a large dining room and a huge, well-equipped kitchen with a walk-in freezer and refrigerator. I could just imagine Ian's delight if he was to work in this facility. The rooms were set up simply and efficiently for 30–40 individuals, with a single bed, hand basin, desk, chair, and chest of drawers.

There was no carpet anywhere, but the polished, honey-colored, natural wood floors and the airy atmosphere gave a warm, glowing feeling to the building. There were recreation rooms inside and tennis courts outside. What more could we ask for? But we did have questions. Was it available? Would they allow us to use the building and all the facilities? How much would it cost?

We met together with the Mother Superior and two other sisters in her office. She told us how the convent had been booked for a three-month retreat by a group of sisters from Europe, but they had just cancelled. Thus, the facility would be vacant for the next three months. Yes, they would be willing for us to use the convent, but only as a residence for girls.

After discussion they agreed to allow us to provide main meals for the male students, also, but they would have to be accommodated elsewhere. So far, so good!

We knew in our hearts that God was fulfilling His promise to work on our behalf. This had to be God's provision. Alan took courage and asked, "How much will it cost?"

The Mother Superior looked at him, smiled, and graciously replied, "Nothing. There will not be a cost."

We sat wide-eyed with astonishment. "But surely there must be some charge," Alan protested.

Again the reply, "No, nothing."

Alan protested again. "We have to pay something for this great facility."

The Mother Superior thought for a moment and then said with a twinkle in her eye, "All right, if you insist, you can pay one dollar per student per week."

We could hardly believe our ears. Thirty dollars a week for the use of the convent! God certainly had prepared a most abundant gift for Vision Bible College. We all stood together in a small circle, joining hands with those dear Catholic sisters. Alan gave thanks and praise to God for the hospitality so generously given.

An ever-increasing crowd of new students greeted us back at Hebron. They began their stay in Vision Bible College by seeing God's miraculous provision on their behalf. Mary moved into the convent along with the 30 single women. The single men and married students stayed at Hebron with us. That night, we rejoiced with a great celebration meal together at Hebron.

CHAPTER 23

Is It The Time?

*"To everything there is a season,
a time for every purpose under heaven."
Ecclesiastes 3:1*

"I want this sort of television program in Australia and I want you to be involved in it."

This startling word came to Alan as he was sitting in the TBN studio in California in the summer of '76. Jim Spillman had invited him to be a guest on Channel 40's *The Praise the Lord* program he was guest hosting. After Alan's part was over, he sat in the studio watching the whole procedure of putting a television program to air and it was then that he felt the Lord asking him to be involved in Christian television. Bear in mind, at that time there was hardly any Christian television in Australia.

Interestingly, a year earlier I had been asked to participate in a women's television program during one of The Temple Trust trips to America. I became aware of the enormous potential of television and began to sense God saying that this was also what He wanted in Australia.

During the rest of his time in America that summer, Alan viewed Christian television programming with a new interest.

Involvement, he began to realize, was going to be no small miracle. God would really have to be in it.

The Temple Trust Board of Directors, as Alan shared the vision with them, felt exactly the same way. In fact, it took the Board a whole three months of prayer and discussion before they finally, in November 1976, came to the conclusion that this was the direction the Lord wanted them to go. Plans for television were announced at the conference in January 1977.

"It will take us two years of preparation," Alan said, explaining something of the enormity of going into a television ministry. At the time, even he himself didn't appreciate what a mammoth undertaking it would be and how many battles and disappointments lay ahead before the final breakthrough.

It was with tremendous, almost naïve, enthusiasm that a group of six men visited the USA in August 1977 especially to study Christian television. They included Murray Cameron, Gordon Gibbs, Syd Polley, and Alan.

On the trip there seemed to be a real possibility of working with The 700 Club, a Christian television program founded and directed by Pat Robertson. They came away from their visit to The 700 Club greatly enthused and convinced that this was the kind of program needed in Australia.

While there was an obvious need to produce an Australian-oriented program, Alan could also see the distinct advantage of being linked with an international ministry so that, as an organization, they could be looking beyond the shores of Australia and be part of a global strategy for evangelism.

When they returned to Australia, there was great anticipation as to how things were going to open up. In the meantime, The Temple Trust, in conjunction with Christian Television Association (CTA), had been working on a pilot for a half-hour children's program incorporating puppets, Bible stories, and larger-than-life-sized animals.

The pilot was made on December 13, 1977. There was much excitement as to how it would be received by Channel 9. Then suddenly, as if a bubble had been pricked, all projected television plans fell through. The children's program was rejected. Plans to work with The 700 Club failed to materialize as local TV stations thought it was too American.

By January 1978, a whole year of the projected two-year plan had passed and apart from gaining much valuable experience, we were apparently no further ahead. Then, just as we had come to the end of ourselves and our own natural resources, a new development took place.

In January, quite unexpectedly, Alan received a letter from the PTL Club in Charlotte, North Carolina, asking if The Temple Trust would be interested in being its representative in Australia. Alan had previously written to the PTL Club seeking their help, but had received no response. The PTL Club, as it turned out, had been looking for a contact in Australia and a pastor from Melodyland Christian Center had recommended they get in touch with Alan. In March, at the opening of the new ministry office, God gave further confirmation that this was indeed the way He was leading.

Following his message at the opening of our new offices in Bondi Junction on March 5, Jim Spillman of Omega Fellowship in Anaheim, California, and guest speaker for the occasion, gave an interesting prophecy regarding television.

"The television stronghold has already been broken down and all you have to do is march through the breach. There has been a great wall that has kept organizations and ministries out—one so high that you can't see over it. But that wall has been breached by someone else and they are inviting you and your whole company to walk through that breach. It is done!"

Wasn't that just what had happened with the PTL Club? It wasn't Alan who had approached them, but they who had written to him. With this in mind, later that year in July, Alan and I visited America enroute to the international Anglican Charismatic conference in Canterbury, England, and arranged to visit the PTL Club in Charlotte.

On our way we stopped off at Los Angeles to stay with Jim Spillman in Anaheim and while there, invited Jim's co-pastor, the singer Willie Murphy, to come with us to Charlotte. Willie was very well known to the PTL staff, having appeared on the program on a number of occasions.

His presence was invaluable. Acting as an ambassador, he was able to introduce us right into the hub of PTL life. A meeting with Jim Bakker, the founder and host of the PTL Club, looked like an impossibility. We talked with the senior executives over lunch and shared the vision for Christian television in Australia. They were able to arrange for us to be on the PTL Club program being filmed that night at Heritage USA. We were warned we would have no longer than eight minutes to share.

Later that evening, excited and rather nervous, we were ushered onto the PTL Club set in the amphitheater. Under the glare of television lights and cameras, we met Jim Bakker for the first time.

"Is it time for Christian television in Australia?" Jim Bakker asked in a loaded opening question.

With only minutes left on that section of the program, and realizing that his answer could affect any further relationship we might have with the PTL Club, Alan gave his reply everything he had.

"Absolutely," Alan replied, his voice sounding strong and confident. "We need Christian television in Australia and we need it now."

With the precious minutes ticking away, he went on to passionately share from the depths of his heart. The result was that by the end of the program, Jim Bakker had virtually agreed for the PTL Club to go on television in Australia.

It really did appear as if a breach had been made and a way prepared to march through. But, as Alan was soon to discover, the continuing faith battle for establishing a Christian television program in Australia was far from over.

Following the 1979 conference, Alan and board member Don Baker went to Charlotte to further develop the relationship with the PTL Club. Financial support was forthcoming and during the next year, pilot programming was developed and recorded at the Channel 4 Studios in Wollongong, Australia. But once again, it was not acceptable to the TV stations. By the end of 1979, the vision for a Christian television show had not materialized despite all the efforts that had been made. So, in early 1980, in preparation for another pilot, another team planned to visit the United States and shoot some footage that could be used in the show.

At this stage, Alan was greatly helped by two experienced television cameramen who had recently become Christians. However, when applications were made for business visas to visit America, they were turned down. Alan, contrary to his normal nature, wrote a strong letter to the U.S. consulate in Sydney explaining that this refusal amounted to religious discrimination. As a result, he was invited to meet with the U.S. Consular General, his deputy and the woman who gave oversight to the visa application. They explained the refusal was because labor unions in America wouldn't allow us to bring cameras into the country to do filming. They were, however, granted visitor's visas.

The trip involved stops in a number of cities. A few days before we arrived in Charlotte, Jim Bakker decided to take some key staff away for a leadership retreat. So Alan, who was to have been a guest on the program, instead was asked to host the American PTL Club program in Jim's absence. C. M. Ward, an Assembly of God radio revivalist, was the main guest and two of the Australian team, Pastor Gordon Gibbs and gospel singer Robert Coleman, also participated.

After the show was over, the PTL Club producer, Bill Gaithwaite, said to Alan, "Why don't we produce the Australian program right here in the studio in Charlotte?"

Alan was all for it and within a month they were producing an Australian version of the PTL Club in the same studio and using the same desk that Jim Bakker used for the American program. The PTL Club was extremely generous, supplying all the resources and the finances to make it all happen. We often shared the same guests that were there for the American program. Alan and I sometimes hosted the program together.

During 1980, we produced thirty one-hour shows and later in the year we went on our first station in Australia, Channel 4 in Wollongong, which was also beamed into the southern suburbs of Sydney. So, at long last the dream, the vision of Christian television, was coming into being.

Later on, when we thought all was going well, a misunderstanding arose when the PTL Club Vice President for world missions thought Jim Bakker wanted Alan out of hosting the Australian PTL Club program. Coming to Australia in January 1981, he demanded to meet with The Temple Trust Board of Directors and required Alan to resign his position.

Initially, Alan wouldn't do it. He had given nearly four years of "blood, sweat and tears" to get this far and he wasn't about to step down.

Wrestling with all this, Alan went for a walk on a country road and, staring down at the gravel beneath his feet, he cried out to God, "I can't believe this is happening. Why is this being taken from me when we have only just begun? You promised we would be on Christian television. I don't understand what You are doing God. Why did You open the door, only to close it again in my face?"

Eventually, reluctantly, knowing that it was the PTL Club that was completely financing this venture, Alan agreed to step down. "It's the hardest thing I've ever had to do in ministry," he said, his voice choked with grief.

Years later, when he visited Jim Bakker in prison in Rochester, Minnesota, Jim told him that he had not wanted Alan to resign. Looking back, however, we could see that God was protecting Alan, pulling him out of his involvement with the PTL Club before its leadership crumbled. Previously, during our visits to Charlotte, Alan and I had been aware of certain shortcomings in the PTL Club ministry that caused us concern. Alan used to say, "If God can do all this with the ministry as it is, what could He do if they got their act together?" Nevertheless, Alan has always had a deep sense of gratitude for all that Jim Bakker did for him and the television ministry in Australia.

So, the dream of television had to die. It was the death of a vision. At the time, Alan had no idea that, years later, under totally different circumstances, in a new place, with people he did not yet know…the dream would be resurrected.

A NEW DAY

CHAPTER 24

The Seed Has To Die

"Except a corn of wheat fall into the ground and die, it abideth alone . . ."
John 12:24 (KJV)

Cuddles, as her name suggests, was an adorable, black, female guinea pig with white and tan markings. She and 11-year-old Joy were inseparable. It was a common sight to see Joy walking around Hebron with the furry bundle snuggling into her neck. Whenever we went near her cage, Cuddles came out of her bed in the hay chirping and making loud gurgling sounds in her throat. She wanted someone to pick her up all the time.

One day I noticed that one of her paws was swollen and infected. She may have caught it on some wire. Over the next few days, instead of healing, the sore became worse and her foot more swollen. I decided to take Cuddles to the vet.

"It's touch and go," he said. "These little animals don't live very long and when there is infection they can go down very quickly."

On my return home we bathed her foot to draw out the poison, wrapped it in a bandage and administered much prayer. We really believed that God would heal her.

A few days later on Friday, June 30, 1978, the day before Alan and I were due to leave on a major overseas trip, Joy ran into my bedroom. "Mummy, come and look at Cuddles, there is something wrong with her, she's lying on her side and won't get up."

Joy's eyes were already filling with tears and I knew that Cuddles was very ill.

"Stay here a moment, Joy," I said, trying to hide the fear in my voice.

I hurried into the sunroom where we kept Cuddles' cage. I put my hand into the hay and lifted her little body out of the cage. To my horror, I realized she was dying as I was holding her, even though I was praying urgently that she would be healed. Life had almost left her and the stillness of death was taking over. My heart sank.

"Oh God, she's dead," I whispered. I could feel the pain and fear as I heard myself speak the words. "Oh God, what am I going to tell Joy?" I cried out in desperation. Immediately God gave me the answer.

"Tell her I will redeem it. Tell her all things work together for good to those that love God and are called according to His purpose."

I felt the peace and presence of the Lord fill my heart and mind. That was very reassuring, but how could I tell Joy that Cuddles was dead? She would be broken hearted and giving her that promise might not bring much comfort right now. I gently laid Cuddles' lifeless form back into the bed of hay and with a heavy heart, made my way back to the bedroom. Joy was sitting on the edge of the bed, tears streaming down her cheeks.

It was one of the hardest things I've ever done, to form the words in my mind and speak them out aloud, "Cuddles is dead, sweetheart."

Together we went back to the sunroom. I felt so helpless. Then God reminded me what He had told me to tell her.

"We can't understand why she wasn't healed, but God said to tell you that He would redeem this and turn it to good for you, Joy," I said tearfully. I held her close to me and we cried together.

"Can we bury her in the garden?" Joy asked through her sobs and tears.

Alan went to find a spade. Together we went outside and found Cuddles' favorite spot under a tree. Joy had often put her out there in her run to nibble the green grass.

"I want to hold her once more," Joy said with a lump in her throat.

I took the little lifeless body and carefully wrapped her in the baby blanket Joy used to put under her when she took her out of the cage. One last loving hug and then she was laid to rest on a bed of clean hay in the ground. Alan prayed a simple prayer and the little burial service was over.

My heart was in agony at the thought of leaving Joy the very next day to be away on an overseas trip for three weeks. I felt a wrenching and anguish deep inside. Every instinct and emotion of my mother's heart yearned to stay to love and comfort Joy, but I knew without a doubt that God wanted me to go with Alan to America and England. The reassuring fact was that Joy, in childlike faith, had taken firm hold of the

Lord's promise that Cuddles' death would work for good. I could see the light of that hope in her eyes.

The next morning when we were ready to leave for the airport, Mum and Dad came out to the front porch with Beth and Joy to say goodbye. We hugged and kissed each one. Mum patted me on the shoulder and said reassuringly, "She'll be all right. We will take care of her."

Joy was crying as I held her. She knew I didn't want to leave her but by the grace of God she had been able to release me to go. I kissed her moist cheek and whispered gently. "I love you sweetheart. We'll believe together that God is going to turn this to good."

There was a lump in my throat and tears in my eyes when we turned to give one last wave from the car as we were driving off.

I knew that Dad (or Grandpop, as the girls called him) would soon be able to bring a smile to their faces. A walk to the corner store to pick their favorite ice blocks would work wonders.

On the way to the airport I mused quietly to myself. Resurrection, life out of death, was a subject God had been speaking about for months. Although I couldn't explain it in words, I knew I was going through some sort of travail. God wanted to bring something to birth but first there had to be death. What we were living through with the death of Cuddles was a parable of what God was going to do with The Temple Trust, although no one realized it at the time.

At the airport Alan was dictating some last-minute letters to Anne, his secretary. One concerned the Jesus '79 Conference to be held in January that was to be spread over three weeks. "These three weeks will change the rest of your life," he said.

Immediately God had my attention. I knew He was speaking those words directly to me. As Alan and I walked toward the boarding gates I told him, "I believe God was speaking to us when you said 'These three weeks will change the rest of your life.'"

Alan replied thoughtfully, "Yes, I feel you're right."

Little did we know just how right that was going to be.

As it turned out the trip was one of the most significant we had ever made. One highlight was our visit to the PTL Club. Another was parti-cipation in the Anglican International Conference for Spiritual Renewal held at Canterbury, England.

Canterbury was a historic city with narrow streets and quaint shops. Right in the heart of town was old Canterbury Cathedral where the final service of the conference was being held. Alan was one of only eight non-Anglican participants and was invited to briefly address the conference.

On Tuesday night we heard Reverend Terry Fullham from the U.S.A. give his message, "The flower fades when the spirit blows." The theme was "Life Out of Death." He said one of the works of the Holy Spirit is to breathe death upon all human flesh. It is true that God breathed life into the dead bones (referring to Ezekiel's valley of dry bones), but before the renewing power of the Spirit is possible there must first come the destroying blast of the hot breath of God. He was speaking of religious activities and organized religion, but both Alan and I began to sense an application to our own lives.

Then, at the Festival of Praise on Saturday night at Canterbury Cathedral, Archbishop Coggan spoke of death. "I am looking for the death of the Charismatic movement," he said, explaining that it had to die as an independent movement and be incorporated into the church.

Colin Urquhart, the main speaker, made reference to death when he prophetically declared that there were people present that night who would face martyrdom because of their faith.

His words did not dampen the enthusiasm of those present. To them the meeting was a great climax to a wonderful week and they expressed their joy and praise with great exuberance at every opportunity. By contrast I was sad, depressed and miserable. I felt as though I was at a funeral instead of a festival. My desire was to leave the excited crowds and find a quiet, lonely place to weep, but I stayed and cried silently deep down inside. I couldn't work out what was wrong with me. Perhaps the Holy Spirit within me was giving witness to something my conscious mind was not yet able to comprehend.

The conference came to an end. It was time to say goodbye to friends, old and new. We shared with them how the next part of our journey would take us to a place called Watford where we would attend a seminar on TV production at the J. Arthur Rank Foundation Studios. Someone asked, "How are you going to get there?"

We answered with a smile, '"We have prayed and asked the Lord that same question, seeing as we have no car. The Lord seems to be saying not to worry, everything is in His control. We don't know where we are going to sleep tonight and we have no idea how we are going to get to Watford."

The editor of our ministry magazine, June Coxhead, who was spending her holiday in England and also attending the conference, spoke up. "I'll take you," she offered, "but before I take you to Watford, first let me stop on the way at the hotel where my mother is staying and tell her what we are doing."

We loaded our bags into June's car and began the drive south toward our destination. Conversation between the three of us was interesting. June had a number of questions on how to receive God's guidance. We shared with her the principles we had learned from scripture and from our own experience. Time went by fast and it wasn't long before we pulled up outside the hotel where June's mother was staying. June led the way into the hotel lounge room and suggested we have a cup of tea. We sat down on a comfortable sofa and took out our map. The subject of our conversation was about how we could get to Watford and where we could stay.

Sitting opposite us on the other side of the dark-stained coffee table was a couple also drinking tea. Suddenly the man broke into our conversation, "I couldn't help hearing you mention Watford. We live in Watford, can we help you?"

Three pairs of eyes looked up from the map and stared at the man across the table. Could they help? It was obvious to Alan, June and I that it was no coincidence that this man and his wife from Watford were sipping tea in the lobby of that hotel at exactly same time we were there, discussing how we would get to Watford. June's questions about guidance were certainly being answered in a very practical way.

The couple had just dropped in for a cup of tea on their way home and when we explained our situation they offered to drive us to Watford and find a place for us to stay. They took us home for more tea and something to eat and then drove us to a small, appropriately named hotel, The Southern Cross, a quaint establishment owned by an Australian lady. We were given a small, modest room furnished simply with a double bed, chair, dresser and hand basin. On Sunday night we went to bed as usual. The next day we would begin the television school study course.

It was 4 a.m. Monday morning when Alan woke, immediately aware of a tremendously heavy sense of pressure weighing him down. He had never experienced anything like it in his life. He paced up and down our small room like a caged lion rebuking what he thought must be some kind of satanic attack.

For the next 36 hours he felt a great pressure bearing down on him, as though he was trying to hold up the whole world. At first, he wondered if he had done what some people said every Charismatic would eventually do, go over the edge and crack. He didn't know if this intense pressure was coming from the devil or the Lord. He could hardly sleep or eat, nor could he concentrate on the TV course we were studying.

Eventually, Alan began to realize that God was in it. It was our last evening in England before returning home to Australia. Alan was still restless and decided to go for a walk while I did some last minute packing. He went for a walk through a nearby park in the twilight of the beautiful, English summer day. Leafy branches were overhanging the pathway as he walked. Then, as it had happened to the disciples on the road to Emmaus, suddenly it seemed Jesus joined him and they walked together down the path. The Holy Spirit spoke gently to his heart.

"Alan I want you to lay The Temple Trust on the altar and let it die."

Back to his mind came John 12:24, *"Unless a grain of wheat falls into the ground and dies, it remains alone; but if it dies, it produces much grain."* In the presence of Jesus he couldn't say no and only wanted to say yes. The glory of God was there and Alan knew he had no other desire but to please Him.

"It's your ministry," he said, "You gave it to us in the first place. It's Yours to take back. Now I willingly give it back. Lord, take it."

That was a divine encounter and Alan knew it. The Temple Trust was to die. Strangely, right from the start, Alan had sensed the significance of seven years. Seven years would be up on the following January. It was with a sober heart that Alan returned to our hotel room that night and shared what had taken place in the park. He said, "God wants The Temple Trust to die, just like a seed planted in the ground."

"The Temple Trust is to die," I repeated, a little taken aback. But then I understood. That was why God had been speaking to me about death for so long. Then there was Cuddles' death and all the messages about death at the conference. Obviously, God was speaking to both of us very clearly, but it was hard to comprehend. These last eight years had been so exhilarating we were hardly able to catch our breath. It had been like sitting on the edge of a huge wave pushed forward by the incoming tide of the Holy Spirit pouring into Australia.

"Lord, You want us to put it all on the altar and let it die? What does this mean? We have our biggest conference planned for January 1979. What are we to do now?"

CHAPTER 25

Life Out of Death

". . . but if it die, it bringeth forth much fruit."
John 12:24 (KJV)

Two days later back in Australia, that sense of unease and restlessness was still with Alan. The first night he woke up at 3:00 a.m. and, unable to sleep, walked around the nearby streets. Then he decided to go on a prayer drive to the various sites for the Jesus '79 Conference in January. Finally, he felt led to go to a place known as the Gap, which was on the south headland to the entrance to Sydney Harbour. Sad to say, the Gap was literally a place of death. Many unhappy people threw themselves over the high cliff overlooking the ocean onto the rocks far below.

From the headland one could look west and have a beautiful view of the Sydney Harbour Bridge and the city skyline. From the same spot one could turn and look far out over the Pacific Ocean to the eastern horizon.

Here Alan witnessed one of the most spectacular sunrises he had ever seen. Out of the pitch-blackness, first as a tiny speck of orange and then as a glorious splash of yellow, orange, red and gold, burst the sunlight. Although different imagery, it was the same message—light or life coming out of darkness or death. What was God trying to say?

As he walked up and down the headland praying in the Spirit in the glory of that early morning, a simple phrase began to form in his mind, "It's a new day!" He found himself speaking it prophetically out loud over and over. "It's a new day! It's a new day! It's a new day!"

"What do you mean by the death of The Temple Trust?" Allan Alcock, chairman of The Temple Trust Board of Directors, had challenged Alan on his return from England.

At that moment, I happened to drop by the office and was able to join in this significant conversation.

"Is it the death of The Temple Trust as an organization or you having to die to The Temple Trust?" asked Allan.

Alan understood in general terms that God was talking about death, but he hadn't really thought it through. Now Allan was forcing him to be specific.

"Are you prepared to give up the whole ministry if that's what God wants?" Allan asked.

It was a hard question, especially when asked point blank. Alan's mind flashed back over the years of struggle and sacrifice we had experienced, along with the joys and disappointments. Could he give everything up, just walk away and leave it in someone else's hands, especially now that we were beginning to see some real fruit for our labors? Could he? But, if that was what God wanted…

Sitting there behind his executive desk deep in thought, Alan gazed out the window at the panoramic view of the city his office window commanded. "Yes!" he said at last. "Yes I can!"

There and then, in an Abraham/Isaac-type sacrifice, the three of us prayed, and Alan put the whole thing on the altar.

The time came for Alan to share the news about changes in the ministry with the staff. At a staff prayer meeting he talked and prayed. It was with sober faces and tear-filled eyes that the staff listened to Alan's prayer.

"God, I lay down the people, the ministry. God, You are pruning the organization. Even these very offices may have to go so You can bring forth something new. The only way that can happen is for me to put that seed in the ground and let it die."

Alan had mixed feelings. On the one hand, he was excited about what God was doing. On the other hand, he felt concerned for the staff. He realized that they might not understand why this was happening. The changes ahead would affect them greatly.

It was a death and burial as real as the day he, Joy and I had buried Cuddles. As with Joy, Alan believed that new life would come from this decision. But like Joy, too, there was to be a period of waiting, a test of faith.

For years, Joy had wanted a dog. Cuddles, in fact, had been a substitute for that original longing. "Couldn't I have one?" she asked time and again. While Cuddles had been alive that had been impossible, but now Cuddles was dead.

"Alright," Alan and I finally agreed, only we couldn't get it immediately. The school holidays were coming up, visitors were expected and generally it was a very busy time. Also, on September 12, Alan would be leaving to attend the Christian Summit Convocation in Singapore. So a date, September 22, was set for after his return and duly marked on the calendar—the day we were to get the puppy.

Joy knew exactly what she wanted. She'd seen it on television—a white, fluffy poodle. "Can I have one like that?" she asked.

"Well, we'll see. We'll pray about it," I had said. I didn't want to promise something we couldn't get and have Joy be disappointed.

Joy waited impatiently for that very special date to arrive. She knew nothing could happen before then, unless God put one on the doorstep and that was impossible, or was it?

One morning during the school holidays, before Alan had left for Singapore, Joy was rather down in the dumps and was moping around the kitchen.

"Why don't you go and feed the birds under the palm tree?" I suggested.

A few minutes later I heard gleeful shrieks from outside. "Look, Mummy, look!"

I went rushing out and there I was confronted with an excitable, very frightened ball of white fluff. The little poodle puppy had been hiding in a box under the palm tree and ran out to gobble up the bread as Joy had thrown it to the birds. It had no collar and was apparently ownerless.

There followed two weeks of agonized waiting as we made inquiries in the paper and through the local council for the owner. "If no one comes forward in two weeks, the dog is yours," we were told.

Joy was confident. "It's just a test of faith, the answer to my prayer," she said happily.

She was right. In fact, during the following two weeks we had several inquiries about a lost poodle, even a visit from a man who claimed it was his, but neither the mother dog he brought with him nor the newly found puppy acknowledged one another. To Joy's delight, Cindy became ours, an important, very excitable member of the Langstaff family.

But while Joy had seen an answer to her prayers, the test was still on for Alan. Only slowly did he begin to see the implications of what it meant for The Temple Trust to die in order for the promised new life to come forth.

First came the challenge of conferences. The National Charismatic Conferences had almost been synonymous with the name The Temple Trust. After all, it was through the conferences that The Temple Trust had come into being. In many respects the conferences had been the lifeblood of the organization. Could Alan just give them away?

Again, it was a hard decision. If God meant death, that's what He meant. So, the notice went out announcing that after Jesus '79 there would be no more National Charismatic Conferences. The Conference in January 1979 would be the last one of its kind.

Then there was the Bible school. At Alan's first mention of handing over Vision Bible College to someone else, I felt a pang of sorrow in my heart.

"Are you sure?" I questioned.

"Yes," he said emphatically. He went on to explain, "For some time I felt the need to relinquish my role as principal of Vision Bible College. Much like a relay runner, I've taken the college as far as I can go. Now it needs someone with both the time and talent to take up the baton and run with it."

It was obvious Alan had made up his mind and was relieved at the whole idea. By contrast, I felt a rush of emotions and myriad thoughts poured into my mind. I felt a little like a mother being told that one of her children had to be given away. I needed God's grace to release it.

As Alan was praying about what to do, the name "Chant" came to mind. Immediately, he thought of Barry Chant in Adelaide. He didn't even consider Barry's brother Ken, who at that time, besides pastoring a Christian Revival Crusade church, was principal of the Launceston College of Theology. The LCT was a Bible correspondence course offering various certificates and a degree. As far as Alan knew, Ken was firmly entrenched in Tasmania.

In fact, Ken had been feeling a strong stirring for some time to leave Tasmania and move to Sydney, but he had been resisting. It wasn't until he was in Singapore attending the convocation there that the Lord finally got through. Ken realized that if he was going to stay in the Lord's will he had no other choice but to say, "Yes."

He and Alan were flying somewhere between Sydney and Brisbane, returning from the convocation, when Ken shared his decision with Alan. As he began to speak, Alan could hardly believe what he was hearing. There was not a shadow of doubt in his mind that here beside him sat the new VBC principal.

It was arranged that in December, Ken, his wife Alison, and three of their children, Sharon, Eric and Baden, would move up to Sydney and into the residence at Hebron, which would again become the headquarters for VBC. They would also set up offices there for their correspondence school. For this to happen, we had to move out.

Although originally purchased exclusively for the Bible college, as the student body had grown and new accommodation needed to be found, Hebron had become a community household comprised of the Langstaff family and a group of about nine single people, including The Temple Trust Task Force.

At the time of moving, everything was full steam ahead for the three-week Jesus '79 conference in January, the biggest Charismatic Conference The Temple Trust had ever tackled. As Alan had already stated, it would be the last conference of its kind.

It was with a certain amount of nostalgia and awe when, after weeks of preparation, hours of prayer, fasting and some big steps of faith, we finally stood up on the rostrum that sunny Sunday afternoon on January 14. Alan addressed a colorful crowd of 10,000 arrayed before him on the steps of the Sydney Opera House. Many had umbrellas up to protect them from the sun and others had handkerchiefs covering their heads.

"I believe we are standing at the crossroads of church history, as far as the Renewal is concerned," Alan announced to the crowd. "We are ending one era and entering another."

Alan went on to outline the seven signs, or characteristics, of this "New Day" that God had given him at the Gap. First, the miraculous would become more commonplace. Then there will be a ten-fold growth and increase among the people of God. Unusual miracles would take place among God's people. New ministries would be released, especially the ministries of Ephesians 4:11. Also, women's ministry, spiritual warfare, and prayer and intercession would increase. There would be new love and unity in the Body of Christ. Finally, the glory of God would be manifest in the people of God (Isaiah 60:1-2).

Not only did we stand at a crossroad in church history, but we were at a significant turning point in the spiritual history of Australia as a nation. Alan had worked with Tom Hallas, the new Australian Director of YWAM, who had been given keen insights into the wounded spirit of Australia. He traced this wounded spirit back to the formation of Australia as a penal colony. The nation had been born in rejection. As Tom Hallas wrote,

> *"Britain's motivation was that she was rejected as an authority by the North American States and thus had nowhere to dump her socially rejected. Australia, therefore, became a convenient place to unload the rejected. That is if they survived the 19,000-kilometer journey. Some chose the gallows rather than face the horror of exile.*
>
> *It is clear then, that this nation was born in rejection. The only way that Australians have been able to anesthetize themselves from the insecurity that resulted has been to pursue a course of independence from God maintained only by material acquisition."* [1]

In the introduction of *An Anzac Story,* Bryce Courtenay describes Australia in these insightful words:

> *"We are a nation founded in misery and despair, the unwanted children of a Mother England who declared us thieves, whores and misfits and threw us out of her house, sending us to the far ends of the earth into exile where it was hoped we might be forgotten."* [2]

That might have been Britain's hope and plan, but the God of hope had not forgotten or rejected Australia. John Dawson writes of Australia in his book, *Taking Our Cities For God:*

> *"Whole countries are kept in darkness by satanic lies that have become cornerstones of a particular culture. Take, for example, the struggle with rejection and the fear of authority experienced by many Australians, because their country originated as a penal colony. Entering through these cruel roots of*

Australian history, Satan has been able to create a general distrust of all authority figures, including the highest of all who is, of course, God Himself.

The truth is that Australia is not a nation founded on rejection and injustice, but a chosen people with as much dignity and potential as any people in history. They are a people greatly loved by a heavenly Father who is calling them to healing and purpose." [3]

On Tuesday night at the conference, God used Loren Cunningham to bring a timely message on forgiveness. He emphasized our need as Australians to forgive Britain and be healed from the spirit of rejection that had dominated our nation. John Dawson describes what happened that night following Loren's message:

"In Sydney in 1979 I witnessed an interdenominational gathering of fifteen thousand believers making a covenant with God on behalf of their nation. There was spiritual release when one leader led the crowd to extend forgiveness toward Britain for the injustice suffered by their forefathers in the establishment of Australia as a penal settlement." [4]

That leader was Alan. How amazing that God could use a man born under a spirit of rejection for this moment of destiny!

Looking back on this historic moment, John Dawson wrote:

"Prophetic revelation about the purpose and destiny of the nation has been pouring into Australia through its national church ever since. Australian Christians have begun to discover many indicators of God at work even in the earliest days of their national history, and they are filled with faith concerning the future." [5]

The theme of healing of relationships and forgiveness was continued with Francis McNutt's message on the Thursday night. Both messages were followed by deep, personal ministry, and on Thursday night, by a very meaningful foot-washing ceremony. In some cases, whole families were reconciled and very deep wounds were healed. One woman, who had suffered in a Nazi prison camp to the extent that she couldn't even recall the face of her own mother who had died in the camp, came through into a beautiful release. The next day the very change in her countenance told the story. Only eternity will reveal all that God had done.

As His love permeated the huge crowd on those nights, hearts overflowed with praise and gratitude. I raised my eyes toward heaven, seeing the twinkling of stars against the dark night sky. I lifted my hands and voice, joining in the praise.

I will give thanks to Thee, O Lord, among the people.
I will sing praises to Thee among the nations.
For Thy steadfast love is great,
Is great to the heavens,
And Thy faithfulness, Thy faithfulness to the clouds.
Be exalted, O God, above the heavens.
Let Thy glory be over all the earth.
Psalm 108:3-5 (RSV)

It seemed that heaven was touching earth in an unforgettable way.

Everyone was very conscious that it was God and not man who was in control of this conference. This was evident even in the weather. In the week prior to the international conference, Sydney had suffered a severe heat wave. The week following there were some heavy rainstorms, but for the week of the conference, God kept the rain at bay. Just to demonstrate what a miracle that was, on Wednesday night, the only night there wasn't an open-air rally at the Randwich racecourse, it rained.

At the concluding rally on Friday night, "Mr. Pentecost," David du Plessis, brought all this to a final challenge in the words of Mary. "Whatever He (Jesus) says to you, do it."

Tom Hallas's message on the wounded spirit of Australia, coupled with Alan's message, "It's A New Day," set against the background of the Jesus '79 Conference, was made into a film by the Australian Religious Film Society.

What Alan didn't share at the time of the conference was how the Lord was challenging him personally. When Alan had first been challenged with the death of The Temple Trust, he had thought of it basically in relationship to himself—him leaving and someone else taking over the helm. What he had never considered was a cessation of the whole organization itself—at least in the form it had been operating. But gradually God's plan had been coming clearer.

Up until now, the role of The Temple Trust had been clearly defined. Its task had been to promote the Charismatic Renewal. Now, while that was to continue, God was wanting to bring a whole new emphasis—that of evangelism.

We believed one way that God wanted to express that was a change of name. In the scripture, when God wanted to indicate a change of role or direction in a person's life, he had done so by changing their name—Abram to Abraham, Jacob to Israel, Simon to Peter, and Saul to Paul. God wanted to do the same thing with The Temple Trust.

We realized a change of name means a certain loss of identity. It took the Board of Directors some months before they came to a decision to call the new work Vision Ministries. Finally, in April the news was announced. The Temple Trust, as such, had ceased to exist. Vision Ministries had been born. It was the beginning of a new day.

At this point the full implication of this change was still unknown, but one thing was certain. Death of The Temple Trust, as it was for Joy with Cuddles, was not the end, only the beginning of another season of God's purpose and blessing.

CHAPTER 26

Leave All and Go

"Now the Lord had said to Abraham, 'Get out of your country, from your father's house, to a land that I will show you.'"
Genesis 12:1

It had been hard to break up our Hebron community household. That was another area of death for us, as we had grown very close to each other. Hearts were heavy when we realized that God was again stirring up our nest. Now there would be three households: the young women, the young men, and the Langstaff family. We had lived with other people for seven years. It would be very strange to be just a family of four again.

Alan went hunting for a house to rent. He came back excited, obviously pleased with himself. He had found a charming, furnished, two-story terrace house back in the Waverly area. It was only a short distance away from the girls' school and the shopping center. It was owned by a university professor who was going on a six-month sabbatical to America. The lease was not as long as we would have liked, but it would be a start.

"I think you will really like it," Alan said reassuringly.

Alan knew me well and he was right. Our new home on Wiley Street was charming. It was a restored terrace row house with a bright yellow front door and a "pocket-handkerchief" garden. Downstairs was a gracious living room with French doors opening on to the brick-paved area that led to the back garden. The tiny kitchen had a stable door leading outside. It was well equipped and had bright green countertops and cupboards—the only thing in the house that was not to my liking. Upstairs were three bedrooms and a bathroom separated by small landings and stairs. Our bedroom looked like a picture from a decorator's magazine. Antique-scrubbed furniture and a small, moss-green, velvet love seat gave Old-World charm and a touch of nostalgic ambiance. Pleated ivory curtains framed two sets of French doors opening onto a narrow terrace with old lace-work iron railings and a wooden floor. Yes, this would be a good place to be for a while.

We were surprised that the adjustment back to a family of four was harder than we expected. There was much joy being together, although we found it more difficult at times. I had become used to sharing my life with so many people, and missed the meaningful relationships that had been formed. Alan had been very busy with the office and ministry, as well as traveling a great deal. Now, it was obvious that the Lord wanted us to relate together and connect in a more meaningful way again as husband and wife, and as a family.

We didn't realize that the recent pruning of relationships and community activities was a preparation for a major change in the near future. As we adjusted to life in a single-family dwelling, we began to get a desire for a permanent home of our own. Several times visiting speakers had given me a prophetic word about the Lord planting us in our own house. We had moved no less than eight times. It would be a refreshing change to settle somewhere. Wiley Street was quiet and tree-lined, with rows of charming old houses that had been carefully renovated. As we walked Cindy, our little poodle, we peered longingly into the lighted windows and imagined ourselves living in one of the quaint homes.

It was with excitement and great interest we noticed a For Sale sign in the front of a house on an adjoining street. We made inquiries with the realtor and arranged to look through it. It was love at first sight for all of us. It had a similar plan and style to Wiley Street, but much smaller dimensions—a real doll's house. What it lacked in size it made up for with charm and atmosphere. We didn't have much money, but then that wasn't a real problem. We had learned that if God guides and it was His will, He would also provide. We slept on it, prayed and decided we would try to buy it. We didn't have to wait long to know God's will on the matter. When Alan called the realtor the next day, the house had been sold.

So, what now, God? There must be a better place for us. The six-month lease was almost up on our terrace house. Perhaps this was the right time to sell our holiday house at McMasters Beach so we could put a deposit on a home in the Waverly/Randwick area. We continued to look at houses for sale and found just what we wanted in Randwick, not far from Hebron.

It was another charming house with ivy-covered walls and a private, paved terrace off the living room at the front. It was a very comfortable restored home with arches separating the family dining room from the kitchen and the living room. French doors opened onto a sunny porch at the back, which led to a small garden. This was just right for us.

The owners of the house were moving a few streets away. Things began to look as though they would work out, but before we could arrange to buy it, the owner changed her mind. She no longer wanted to sell; she would only rent it to us. As our lease was almost up, it seemed we had no other choice but to take it for rent. Alan and I asked ourselves, *What is God saying to us? Are we making a mistake in trying to buy a house?*

We moved in June 1979 into the house on Farnham Avenue. We made a decision to use some of the money from the sale of our holiday home to buy some decent furniture and make a large donation for the television ministry. For so long the girls had had bits and pieces of old furniture, now maybe we could let them choose a bedroom set they really wanted. Joy, 11 years old, chose a very elegant white, Queen Anne-style set. On the other hand, Beth, 18, wanted her room to look more like a study. She chose a light pine wood desk, drawers and divan. Our parents approved of our new home and were happy to see us settled at last. Our two cats, Fluffy and Buffy, and our little dog, Cindy, approved also.

That same month, Alan was invited by Dr. Yonghi Cho, who pastors the largest church in the world, to come to Seoul, Korea to preach for a week. In 1977, Dr. Cho had been the main speaker at the Assembly of God National Conference in Melbourne where Alan was also one of the speakers. During that conference, to Alan's surprise, he found himself scheduled to preach on Sunday morning at Richmond Temple, sharing the pulpit with Dr. Cho. Alan spoke first and then Dr. Cho. That was how they first met.

When Alan was in Seoul, he had an encounter with the Lord where he felt God was calling him to be "committed to grow" beyond what he had experienced to this point. Little did he realize that for this to happen, it would mean a radical step of faith into an unknown future.

The time in Dr. Cho's church left an indelible mark on Alan as he saw first hand what God was doing in this remarkable church. He was also honored to be invited to join the Board of Directors of Church Growth International, which over the years would bring him in contact with leaders from around the world.

We barely had time to settle into our new home before it was August and time for Alan and me to go to Minneapolis, Minnesota in America. As a result of a trip to Singapore in 1978, where he had given a major message at The Summit Convocation, Alan had been invited to speak at the 1979 International Lutheran Conference on the Holy Spirit.

Alan's secretary, Anne, and his administrative assistant, Lynnette, accompanied us to the airport. We parked the car next to the curb and Alan and the girls unloaded the bags and went on ahead into the terminal. I gathered my remaining belongings and stepped out of the car onto the curb. There was excitement in my heart as I anticipated the trip ahead, and I felt the warm sun on my back as I turned to close the car door.

The rear door had been left open and I went to take a step, while at the same time, pushing the door closed with my free hand. All of a sudden my foot hit something very hard and I went hurtling forward over a huge, square, cement planter that had been hidden from my view by the open car door. I sprawled onto the cement pavement, trying to protect myself from the fall. My knees were grazed, my left ankle was badly twisted, and I was somewhat shaken up.

I reminded myself that I was about to go off on a plane and had to get into the air terminal to join Alan. The others were concerned when they found out what had happened. Should I go to the first-aid station? That would take time and we could miss our plane. That didn't seem to be an option. It occurred to me that the devil might be trying to interrupt our trip and prevent me from going to Minneapolis with Alan. I knew my ankle wasn't broken, so I decided to go ahead as planned.

The long flight from Sydney to Los Angeles took about 15 hours. I found it difficult to sleep, but I did have time to pray. Alan was seated on the aisle and I was next to him. My view was limited from that position, looking at the back of the seats in front of me. I could see the passenger in front through a space between the seats. The man was reading a Time magazine, then closed it and laid it on the seat tray in front of him. The cover really attracted my attention. It was a picture of a long board table surrounded by empty chairs. At the head of the table was a chair, obviously belonging to the president, and alongside it an American flag.

As I looked at it I felt a distinct impression from the Lord. "You are going to live under the American flag for a time."

"Oh," I said to myself. "We must be going to visit America sometime and maybe stay for three months or so."

I mentioned it to Alan and didn't think much more about it. We stayed with friends overnight in Los Angeles and then flew to the Twin Cities of Minneapolis and St. Paul.

We stayed at the Curtis Hotel and walked from there to the convention center for the conference. The first Tuesday evening Alan gave the message on "It's A New Day," and it was warmly received. He also had the opportunity to preach at North Heights Lutheran Church, pastored by Dr. Morris Vaagenes. At the time, neither of us realized what a significant trip this was, but we were soon to find out.

We returned to Sydney feeling that our mission was accomplished. It had been our first time to visit the Upper

Midwest and see something of the Lutheran Renewal. We had felt very much at home with the people there.

We enjoyed our new home in Randwick. It was convenient to school for Joy, the bus for Beth, and the ministry office for Alan. It was a comfortable and gracious home, wonderful for family living or hospitality.

My family always celebrated birthdays and special events together. Our home would be an ideal place to celebrate Mum and Dad's golden wedding anniversary. October was a pleasant month in Australia. It would be spring weather, warm enough to open the French doors or sit outside on the shaded terrace. My brothers, John and David, their wives and six children would come. Alan's mother, his brother and wife and four children would also be invited so it would be a full house. It was such a joy to plan and prepare for the occasion. I put together an album with photos and verses, all with a golden theme, and presented it to Mum and Dad at the party. We had a toast and speeches and took many photos. It was truly a wonderful time for us all to share together and a treasured memory for Mum and Dad and each member of the family.

Life continued on as usual until one day in November. It was about 6 p.m. and I had laid the dinner plates out on the kitchen counter. The family was hovering around and I could see through the archway into the family room where the table was set and ready. I began to serve the meal and all of a sudden was overcome by a terrible weight of sorrow and grief. I began to sob.

Alan and the girls were alarmed and wanted to know what was wrong. I didn't know. All I could think of was I felt like someone I loved had just died. Having previously suffered depression and oppression by the enemy, I thought perhaps this was happening again. Alan prayed for me and took authority over the devil and any oppressing spirits. I felt no relief whatsoever. It was obvious that I couldn't continue serving the meal, let alone eat anything. I suggested to Alan that he and the girls eat without me while I went to the bedroom to weep and pray. Beth brought me a cup of tea, thinking it might help.

I lay on the bed and couldn't stop crying. I cried out to God, saying, "What is going on, Lord? I feel as though someone has died and I am grieving over it. Help me, Lord."

After quite some time of continued sobbing, something occurred to me. Maybe God was trying to get my attention to say something in the midst of all this, so I said, "God, if you are trying to say something, please make it clear."

I have always found at critical times like this it is better to say yes to God before you know what He is going to tell you. So, I proceeded by saying tearfully, "I will go wherever You want me to go. I will do whatever You want me to do. I will speak whatever You want me to speak. But I need to know what it is You want. Please make it clear, somehow."

I noticed *Mustard Seeds*, the little book I had been reading, lying on the dresser beside my bed. I picked it up and opened it at random and began to read. The words were describing a woman in a motel taking a shower and how tears of pain, separation and grief mingled with the water as it fell on her face. Immediately I identified with her grief. Her words leapt off the page right into my heart. *"We did it. We really did it. We left the place we love, the people we love, the church we love. We left them all. All thy waves have gone over me, O God.*"[6]

My eyes were riveted to the pages of the book. I read on, only to discover that God had asked the Pulkingtons to leave home and kindred and their ministry in America, to move across the ocean to a different part of the world.

Instantly, as I read those words, I felt a release from the terrible grief of the last two hours. "That must be it," I breathed in astonishment. "You want us to leave everything and move to another part of the world."

I lay there and read the words again. *This is incredible,* I thought. *This is what God is saying.*

I knew without a doubt in my heart that God had spoken. I knew, also, that in some amazing way I had just gone through two hours of the most intense grief I had ever experienced. It was for the same loss that the woman in the book had described. Those feelings of grief, which only a moment ago were overwhelming me, were now instantly replaced with excitement and anticipation.

At that moment, Alan came into the bedroom to see how I was and if God had said anything to me. I looked at his sober, concerned face and said, "I think I know what it is. We have to leave everything and move to another part of the world."

His concerned expression immediately changed to one of astonishment. "But we have only just moved in here," he exclaimed in disbelief. "Where would we move?" he asked.

"I don't know," I excitedly replied. "I just know God wants us to move to another part of the world."

In his mind, Alan did not have any witness one way or another. He didn't understand how anything like this could happen. He certainly wasn't ready to go off and buy tickets to anywhere right now, but to humor me he agreed to pray about it with me. There would have to be clear confirmation from the Lord, changing circumstances, or an open door of some kind.

Not long after this experience, we visited the church that was pastored by one of our board members, Pastor Frank Houston. We found it interesting that his sermon included an illustration of transplanting a tree from a small pot to a large pot to enable it to grow, reach its full potential, and not become root-bound. It was a small thing along the right lines, but certainly not sufficient confirmation for us. I felt sure in my heart it was only a matter of time and God would speak again.

The day after Christmas we drove down the coast to spend time with Alan's mother for her birthday. While there, Beth began to run a high fever and was not feeling well. As we drove home towards Sydney late that afternoon, we could see that we were heading into a very bad storm. Through the windshield of the car I could see the ominous black clouds spreading right across the horizon, and jagged bolts of lightning hitting the ground.

As I looked at this scene before me I heard an inner voice say, "Your life is going to go under a dark cloud for a while."

Little did I realize what that was going to mean.

Beth's condition grew worse and was accompanied by a sore throat, swollen glands, and aches and pains in her body. Even after the initial high fever dropped, she had tremendous fatigue and depression. Three weeks later, after a visit to the doctor and some blood tests, the conclusion was that Beth had some kind of virus similar to mononucleosis and would eventually feel better.

It was the school holidays and we were enjoying our home with its terrace that opened off the living room. Joy often practiced rollerskating there. One day she came in and complained she was too tired to roller skate and was not feeling well. When I came to think of it, I was very fatigued myself. It wasn't long before we realized we both had a fever, sore throats, swollen glands, aches and pains—the same symptoms as Beth had had a few weeks earlier.

Oh, no! I thought. *Whatever this virus is, we have it now.*

Joy, our bubbly, joy-filled 12-year-old, began to feel depressed and suffered extreme fatigue and weakness. I was overwhelmed with fatigue and was so weak I couldn't lift the dinner plates into the kitchen cupboard. Whereas it was our daily pleasure to walk our dog Cindy up the road, now we hardly ever left the house. Beth had to drop out of her classes at Sydney University and Joy had to drop out of school.

The doctor sent all three of us to the infectious diseases hospital for a day to have tests. He wanted to see if the virus could be identified and treated. The specialist had no doubt about our physical condition. We all had a virus. They could see the evidence in Joy's throat, but it was too late to identify. We would all have to rest and wait for recovery, and we were told it could take one or two months or longer!

Beth, Joy and I were too weak to do much but rest. We couldn't go to church, so we had our own special times at home. On Sunday mornings we dressed up and attended church in our living room by watching Robert Schuller's *The Hour of Power*. There was very little Christian television in Australia, so we were thankful we had at least one church service on TV.

At this time, Alan was away in America. He was back in Minneapolis/St. Paul at North Heights Lutheran Church speaking at a Lutheran leadership conference when God spoke to him in a dramatic fashion. Alan was teaching in the Monday afternoon session in the Roseville sanctuary of North Heights Lutheran Church on the subject of "Delegation," and God spoke to him, saying, "You are to delegate the ministry in Australia and move to America."

After the session ended, a Lutheran pastor and his wife from South Dakota came up to him and told him that while he was teaching, they felt a burden to pray for him and they felt God gave them a word for Alan. It was, "You are to train somebody else to take your place."

In other words, he thought. *God is going to replace me.*

Alan's heart leapt with excitement as God was quickly confirming His word. What made it more significant was this couple had not met Alan before and knew nothing of what God had already said. They confessed they were a little apprehensive giving a word to a visiting speaker.

Unknown to Alan, on the previous Sunday I had turned on the TV to get ready to watch Robert Schuller with Beth and Joy. The previous program was just coming to an end when the words on the screen leapt out at me.

"The decision you are about to make will change your life and the lives of your children for many years to come."

God was again speaking to my heart and getting me ready.

On Tuesday morning the phone rang as Alan called me from Morris Vaagenes' home, where the snow now covered the ground in stark contrast to the green grass of our earlier visit. "Something amazing has just happened in my workshop," he said excitedly. He went on to explain, "God has just spoken to me and told me that we are to move to America! I don't know where yet, but God will show us."

"Wow, that's what it's all about. We are to move to America!" I repeated with surprise and excitement. I was awed that God had so sovereignly confirmed His word.

Alan and the team went from the Twin Cities to a conference in Florida, and then on to Charlotte, North Carolina. It was there that the suggestion of producing the

Australian PTL club program in Jim Bakker's studios was made. For Alan, this was a further confirmation regarding moving to America.

The question still remained, where in America were we to move? Even though Charlotte seemed a possibility, Alan didn't feel a witness to it. The team went on to Tulsa where Alan was able to record an interview with Oral Roberts, who provided his own television crew to do it. Then it was on to Seattle, Los Angeles and back through Honolulu to Sydney, all the time asking the question, "Is this the place, Lord? Is this the place?"

I picked up Alan at the airport and we made our way along a stretch of road that led to the freeway. Of course, the main topic of conversation was the word God had given Alan in Minnesota that confirmed what God had spoken to me three months before. As we drove toward our home, the Lord spoke to Alan's heart. "Where the call came is where you are going to live."

So that was the answer. We were to live in Minneapolis/St. Paul, Minnesota. Living under the American flag made sense to us now.

We shared the word with our Board of Directors. They were stunned. First, Alan had said The Temple Trust had to die. Then they changed the name to Vision Ministries. Now he was telling them he wanted to leave Australia altogether. How could this be? As we explained, I wept as I told the board that God was asking me to release the burden of intercession I had carried for the Eastern Suburbs and Body of Christ in Australia.

The board members were not enthusiastic to say the least. It took almost three months before we came into unity and they agreed on the move. However, there was a stipulation. Alan had to find the right person to take his place in Australia.

Then God began to move people around like pieces on a chessboard. Harry Westcott was the man to take over the ministry, but for him to leave his church in Canberra, he needed someone to take his place. Then it became clear that Dan Armstrong was that man. The changeover would take place at the end of 1980.

In the midst of all this, Alan met Jim Spillman in the airport in Sydney as Jim was preparing to fly back to America. Jim had just been ministering in a number of cities around the country and had heard of Alan's desire to move to America. Sitting in the airport lounge, he spoke directly to Alan.

"You are a big fish in a small pond. If you move to America, you will be a small fish in a big pond."

He didn't tell Alan not to do it. He simply asked the question, "Are you sure you really want to do that?"

Alan's answer was, "I don't care if I am a big fish or a small fish, I just want to be where Jesus wants me to be."

Was this a check on Alan's guidance? As if to answer this question, the following Sunday we were again watching Robert Schuller when he told the story of a fish, a goldfish. He said that if you take a goldfish out of a small pond and put it in a big lake, it will grow and grow and grow. Alan realized that God wanted to take us to a new place, Minnesota, the Land of 10,000 Lakes, where we would be out of our comfort zone and could continue to grow. He recalled the word God had given him in Korea about commitment to grow.

After the board's approval, the next step was to apply for permanent visas. Once again they turned down our request. We believed we were to move as soon as possible so the girls could begin school and college in the coming fall. Undeterred by the refusal, Alan went back to the consular's office and met with the same woman he had originally come in contact with in the meeting with the consul general. This time he applied for visitor's visas instead, with the idea that when we arrived in America, we would apply for permanent residency.

Now, this was not the correct way to do it. The woman knew of our plans and could have denied us then and there, making us go through a long procedure in Sydney that could have taken up to a year. For whatever reason, she decided to give us the visitor's visas. We realized God had given us special favor with this lady.

At that time we contacted Morris Vaagenes, and after talking it over with the leadership of his church, he gave his support for our move. Eventually, they sponsored our application to become permanent residents in America and we were forever grateful for their help.

The following weeks were filled with days of hectic activity as we sold or gave away our furniture, had garage sales, and made all the necessary preparation for moving. Joy, of course, wanted to take her poodle with her. So, a crate was made for Cindy for the long journey across the Pacific and on to Minneapolis.

The girls were excited. Beth had previously been given a prophetic word that she would study in America. Joy had been reading the *Little House on the Prairie* books and wanted to live in a place with snow where the Little House on the Prairie stories took place. I had received the original word about moving to another part of the world, and so all of the words and dreams came together. We were literally fulfilling the call that we had received in 1967 to go out like Abraham to a new country and, like Abraham, we went out not knowing what lay ahead of us.

On Sunday, June 8, 1980, our family boarded a Qantas flight to begin a new adventure in a new land. But that's another story that will have to wait for another time.

EPILOGUE

The Langstaff family arrived in Minnesota on June 8, 1980. Alan, Dorothy, Beth and Joy had two suitcases each and their poodle, Cindy. They began a brand new chapter of their lives in a new country—living through new adventures with God, and taking more radical steps of faith and obedience.

There have been many more amazing testimonies of journeys taken, houses provided, ministries founded, and missions accomplished. God has been faithful to them in their new homeland, just as He was to them in Australia.

Both daughters are now married to ministers. Beth graduated from Princeton Seminary with a PhD in Historical Theology, lives in Germany and has two children, Jessica and Jonathan. Joy lives near Alan and Dorothy, works as their administrator, and has four children, Mitchel, Timothy, Hayley, and Benjamin.

Alan and Dorothy now live in a lovely home on a small lake in historic Excelsior, Minnesota, which is on Lake Minnetonka. Gardening has been a special love for them and with the help of others, they have landscaped their property.

In 1984, they founded their own personal itinerant and teaching ministry called Kairos Ministries, Inc. Unexpectedly in 1986, they were sovereignly called to pastor a church in the Twin Cities called Antioch Christian Fellowship. During those 14 fruitful years of ministry, Alan established a Bible school, Dorothy organized a series of conferences, the church developed an extensive missions program, and Alan was actively involved in Christian television, including co-hosting a weekly television program.

For ten years Alan was presiding elder of an international ministerial association with members in 35 countries. In 2005, together with four other ministers, including two other Australians, they established a new international ministerial network called "Omega Team."

In November 2008, Dorothy not only celebrated her 70th birthday, but the completion of this book, *Called Together*. At the same time, Alan and Dorothy celebrated their 50th wedding anniversary. They look back with great gratitude and say, "To God be the glory for the things He has done."

A new book called *A Faith Like Abraham's,* describing their adventures in America, is being planned. They look forward to the future with faith and anticipation, believing that,

"The best is yet to be!"

ENDNOTES

CHAPTER 8

1. Bill and Gloria Gaither, *It Is Finished.*

2. Philip Doddridge, *O Happy Day.*

3. Fanny Crosby, *Rescue The Perishing.*

CHAPTER 9

1. Ralph Mahoney, *Is A New Wave of Revival Coming?* (Burbank, CA: World Missionary Assistance Plan), pages 9-10.

CHAPTER 14

1. Hannah Hurnard, *Hinds Feet on High Places* (London: The Olive Press), page 51.

2. *Hinds Feet on High Places,* page 51.

3. *Hinds Feet on High Places,* page 51.

4. *Hinds Feet on High Places,* page 52.

CHAPTER 25

1. Tom Hallas, "The Wounded Spirit of Australia," *Vision Magazine* 30, (January-February 1979).

2. Ray Kyle, *An Anzac Story,* ed. Bryce Courtenay, (Penguin Group).

3. John Dawson, *Taking Our Cities For God* (Lake Mary, FL: Creation House), page 80.

4. *Taking Our Cities For God,* page 80.

5. *Taking Our Cities For God,* page 80.

6. Betty Pulkingham, *Mustard Seeds* (Hodder and Stoughton), page 100.

Contact Information

Dorothy and Alan Langstaff
Kairos Ministries, Inc.
PO Box 396
Excelsior, MN 55331
USA

E-mail: kairosmin@aol.com

Web: www.kairosmin.org